Influenced

By Destiny

Influenced By Destiny

Marlena E. Neal

PRODIGY
PUBLISHING, LLC

Published by
Prodigy Publishing, LLC
Atlanta, GA 30339
Record_1

Library of Congress Control Number: 2009911975
ISBN 978-0-9824385-0-3

Printed in the United States of America

Dedication

This book is dedicated to my children. I love each one of you very dearly. I hope this book explains why I have high expectations of you and prevents you from experiencing some of the same misfortunes that I have experienced.

Acknowledgements

To GOD Almighty, the Most High, omniscient, omnipotent, and omnipresent Creator for giving me the breath that I breathe and strength to go on when I feel like giving up.

To my children Jada, Joy, Jordan and Jacob for being my motivation.

To my parents for giving me life,

To my Aunt Ann and Uncle John, for everything that you did and accepting me as one of your own.

To Beanie Gooden for always being there for my children when they needed you most.

To Brian and Kimberly Richardson for mentoring me, supporting my family, and being there even when you didn't have to.

To Courtney "Cocoa" Lawson for having my back and reminding me not to settle for less than what I deserve.

To my extended family, Rene Morris and Ether Johnson for accepting me as one of your own.

To my sisters Alicia, Kristen, Aliyah, April, Dannielle for inspiring me.

To my brothers Sean and Theo for being there for me and encouraging me.

To Delano for keeping me grounded, treating me like a lady, giving me hope and most of all, being there for me.

To Jay for the two beautiful blessings you have bestowed upon me and believing in me when I was tired of believing in myself. We have had our ups and downs but I love you no less and wish you the best.

To Raheim Shabazz for all of your help.

To J.L. King for taking time to work with me and all of your input.

To Jarek James for being a lifesaver and for all of the work you put into this project.

To George Sherman and Precious Love for extending your services to me.

To Brian Lassiter for all of your assistance.

To Corrina Moman for holding things down and looking after my girls when people were trying to hold me back. I look forward to our many business ventures together.

To all of my spiritual leaders for blessing me.

To all the historical figures, political figures, entertainers, athletes, etc. for influencing me and impacting my life in more ways than you will ever know.

To everyone that has influenced and been there for me. I love you and will never forget you.

Last but not least to those that hate and conspire against me. May peace be with you even when you are against me.

Foreward

Influenced by Destiny is compiled of personal testimonies from author Marlena E. Neal. The full power of the book is expressed through its profound impact on unadulterated minds, who are ready to implement change into the world in which they live.

Readers will see the common grounds we all stand on as individuals seeking to fulfil our destiny in life. Marlena's struggle against adverse conditions that plague our communities made her courageous and optimistic about her future.

The author's determination to succeed in life represents the response of an African-American woman who does not look at her gender as a disadvantage. Not only does she embrace her womanhood, but she brings critical awareness to the meaning of true sisterhood.

With a writing that is engaging and informative, Marlena E. Neal's inspirational and motivational words will awaken the consciousness of everyone who wishes to seek, find and fulfil their destiny.

Respectfully,

Rahiem Shabazz

Contents

PROLOGUE

A TIME FOR EVERYTHING

Do you have the determination or drive to succeed at something? Well, I am determined and destined to succeed in life. I have been this way from the moment I was conceived and implanted in my mother's womb. I did not know how, I did not know when, and I did not know why. The only thing that I knew, was that I had to succeed in life

Some people are destined to fail, but others like myself, are destined to succeed. I was specifically designed by a Higher Power to persevere and make a difference. I did not know it at first because confusion, frustration, and uncertainty invaded my life from the day that I was born.

Life had never been easy for me. In fact, most people would not believe all the hardships and obstacles that I have managed to overcome. Some of the obstacles that I have encountered were inevitable; others were just a matter of bad judgment. Many people would mistake my determination as having a hard head, but I never saw it that way. I saw myself as having a clear vision and simply having my mind set on what it was I wanted to do. I plan to tell you how I encountered hardship after hardship, obstacle after obstacle, and how I have made one foolish mistake after another, but I hope my story serves an even greater purpose. I hope my story encourages those that need encouragement and influence those that need to be influenced.

Many people may not understand or like my testimony and that is fine because this book is not for everyone. This book is about closure for me and hopefully, it is motivation or words of encouragement for someone else. I do not expect my book to sell millions of copies or heal the world, but I do expect it to touch someone's life so that they can get past whatever it is that they are going through. This book has to be read in its entirety to be fully comprehended and appreciated. This book is a partial reflection of my life and it chronicles some of the events that have made me into the person that I am today. Out of respect for my friends, family and acquaintances, I have changed their names to reserve and respect their privacy. Every chapter of this book represents one year of my life. The title of each chapter has a spiritual meaning behind it.

CHAPTER 1

IN THE BEGINNING

Everyone has a story to tell and I'm no different. My story began when I was born in Detroit, Michigan on March 7, 1980. My father named me Marlena Erica Neal. My initials stood for M.E.N. My father probably knew that men would be one of my biggest issues. I was cute and I was at the center of my parent's attention, at least for the moment. My parents meant the world to me, but like most little girls, it was something about my father that captivated me.

My father was ambitious, articulate, charming, and witty. He had a way with people, especially women, but there was also another side to my father. There was a side to him that I think he rarely discussed or talked about with anyone. This side is a mystery to me, even to this day. My father did not have a real relationship with his biological father, so there was emptiness, a void that lingered inside of him. His relationship with his mother wasn't that much better, but as time went by, old wounds were healed.

My mother was beautiful, clever, independent, strong, and vivacious. Men were attracted to my mother for all sorts of reasons. She was attractive, but she also had a caring spirit. She was the life of any party. My mother also had another side to her that everyone knew about. She had this crazy side that would be your worst nightmare if you allowed it to be. Both of my parents had a quick temper, but people usually stayed as far away as possible from my mother when she was mad because there was no telling what she might do. That crazy side is what frightened most men away from my mother but it was also the same characteristic that managed to attract quite a few men to her. My mother was a good woman with lots of dreams and ambitions. Like most women, she required a lot of attention, love, patience, and understanding. In a sense, both of my parents were looking for something to fill an emptiness that stemmed from their childhood. It is just somewhat unfortunate that, although I managed to inherit some of my parent's best qualities like my father's height and my mother's beautiful bone structure, I also managed to inherit some of their worst qualities like their temper.

I always knew I was different compared to most children. Even at an early age, I was determined to do what I wanted to do. I would stop at nothing to get what I wanted. According to family members, I was crawling, walking, and trying to talk before any other children my age. My mother kept me looking adorable. She worked in the automotive industry at a manufacturing plant. It seemed like everyone wanted to work in a plant years ago because the money was great. That's where she met my father, but when my mother had me, he completed trade school and decided to pursue a career in television.

It seemed like their relationship was over before it even began. My father knew very little about my mother. According to my father, he had no idea my mother already had two kids until the day they brought me home from the hospital. My parents stopped by my aunt's house on the way home from the hospital, that's where he met my sister and brother for the first time. When my father met my sister and brother it came as a complete shock to him because my mother never told him she already had two kids. I guess the more he learned about my mother, the more he realized their relationship wasn't going to work. My parents dated for less than a year. They both eventually went their separate ways. My mother married someone else and so did my father.

My father was actually in a relationship when he met my mother, but like the old saying goes, the grass always looks greener on the other side. There was animosity and resentment between both of my parents. I didn't understand why until I got older. My parents managed to get along well enough to make sure my basic needs were met. My father would come by and visit, but I know that it had to be awkward because my mother's husband was always around.

Charlie, my stepfather was always good to me as far as I could remember, but he and my sister didn't get along that well. I never really knew why. According to my sister, he would make advances at her and my mother never did anything about it. I don't know if it was true or not, but I learned at an early age, never to put anything past anyone, if you know what I mean.

I remember my stepfather reading me bedtime stories and treating me as if I was his very own daughter. I would see Charlie and my mother argue from time to time, but I was too young to think anything of it. My mother locked him out the house a few times and I remember her telling me not to go to the doors or windows, but I didn't pay it any mind.

One day, my stepfather got into a car accident in one of his cars. No one was injured and my mother didn't seem to make that big of a deal out of the whole situation. I remember my mother and stepfather talking about it in the living room like nothing happened. Although my mother didn't seem to make a big deal out of the accident, I knew that at any moment, the slightest thing would cause her to be stressed out and eventually set her off.

People deal with stress differently. Some people drink, some people smoke, some people do drugs, overeat, etc. My mother would often times hold her emotions and frustrations in. At other times, she would be like a ticking time bomb ready to go off at any moment. She never learned how to deal with stress in an effective manner. Generally speaking, a lot of people never learn how to deal with stress and ultimately end up dependent upon alcohol, cigarettes, drugs, etc. My mother eventually became dependent on prescription medication and she would over medicate herself every chance she would get. After seeing how drugs affected my mother, I had a phobia of taking medication.

Everyone has something they depend on when times get hard or when obstacles get in the way. The ironic thing about life is that trials and tribulations are inevitable. Obstacles are often times placed in our way to make us stronger and help us persevere. I believe in giving glory to GOD every chance that I get because GOD is key to helping us make it through. I'm clearly not an expert on religion, but I do embrace all forms of religion. In my opinion, lack of knowledge is the only thing that separates one religion from the next. I am very spiritual and I firmly believe without a doubt that there is a GOD or higher power that sustains us all.

Since my mother wasn't always in the best state of mind and my father was living his own life, I learned certain principles in life the hard way. Some of the principles I have learned involve a set of rules that I used to break through barriers. A barrier is something that we must overcome to persevere. Through trial and error, I learned that when I am faced with barriers, there are basic moral and ethical rules I can live by that help me overcome and breakthrough any barrier that may stand in my way. I have taken the time to list these rules and principles in hopes that someone's life will be touched and they could somehow, some way, find the strength to keep going even when it seems like everything is standing in the way.

How to Break Through Barriers

1. P.U.S.H. (Pray until something happens).

2. Realize that there is always someone that may have it worse than you.

3. Be the best person that you know how to be regardless of the circumstances or obstacles that may stand in the way.

4. Learn how to navigate life's storms.

5. Take control of your destiny.

6. Remind yourself that "failure is not an option."

7. Change the things that can be changed, accept the things that cannot be changed, and ask for wisdom to know the difference between the two.

8. Stay optimistic and never let anyone see you sweat.

9. Learn to forgive and let go.

10. Be thankful that life is only about 10% of what happens to us and about 90% of how we react to it.

All of the principles that I have mentioned were in existence long before I was created or even thought of. I just serve as living proof that despite the barriers that might be standing in your way; you can overcome and make it through. Rather you choose to follow the rules listed above and throughout the remainder of this book will be left entirely up to you. I'm living my life and you have yours to live, but believe me, if I had known then what I know now, I would be a completely different person and so would you.

Life is about choices. We have a choice to do right and a choice to do wrong. No one is perfect. We all fall short of the glory of GOD, but that does not mean we should not try to do what's right. I was told that when you know better, you do better. I am sure my parents tried to do the right thing when they brought me into this world. Unfortunately, things did not work out the way they hoped or probably planned. I don't fault my parents for anything that I went through. I just wish that they would have made better choices or at least tried to make one of their relationships work so that I could have been raised in a more stable environment. Although both of my parents moved on and married different people, I still wonder what my life would have been like if they had managed to stay together.

CHAPTER 2

DOUBLE TROUBLE

Eventually, my mother's marriage to Charlie started falling apart. The two of them split up and got divorced. My mother never managed to have children by Charlie. When the divorce was over, things just didn't seem right around the house anymore. My sister and brother stayed on my mother's bad side, especially my sister. My mother and sister never got along. In my opinion, it was because they were too much a like. My mother made it seem as if my sister and brother were two of the worst children in the whole entire world. They were double trouble in her opinion. I think my mother just resented my sister because she had her at an early age and she wasn't ready to be a single parent,. My mother was no more then 15 years old when she had my sister and from what I was told; she didn't have time to go to the hospital when she went into labor. She gave birth in a bathroom. Later on in life, my sister had the hardest time getting a birth certificate and social security number because there was no official record of her birth. As far as my brother was concerned, I don't know why my mother treated him the way she did. She probably had resentment towards my brother because my brother's father was involved with another woman during the time that he was conceived.

The resentment and anger that my mother had towards my sister and brother was heartrending. There was always an argument or disagreement about something. If it wasn't one thing, it was another. I remember a few of the arguments because some of them usually had something to do with me. One time, I got burned by hot grease because my sister was cooking and the grease splashed on me. My mother was extremely angry and had to take her anger out on someone, so she took it out on my sister. Another time, we were all running around the house and I ran into the wall, so I had to be rushed to the emergency room for stitches.

My sister and brother stayed in trouble according to my mother. She blamed my sister and brother for everything. I would have been in trouble also, but I managed to get away with a lot because I guess my mom felt I was just too young to be punished. I remember my mother yelling and screaming at my sister and brother like she was a drill sergeant. Other times, she was beating the hell out of them. She even sent them to the attic on a few occasions.

I have my share of bad memories, but I also have a lot of good memories from the times I spent growing up with my sister and brother. It's a good feeling having an older sister and brother. I remember staying up late watching the Three Stooges, Sanford & Son and whatever else that came on past my bedtime. I remember getting up watching Fat Albert, Inspector Gadget and all the other cartoons that came on early in the morning.

I remember listening to rap music for the first time and wishing I knew how to break dance. I don't know what it is, but it's something about Run DMC, Salt-N-Pepper, LL Cool J, and Slick Rick that will always stand out in my mind. My sister and brother would listen to the radio and I was right there beside them bobbing my head like I knew what was going on. I didn't know it at the time, but music would definitely have an influence and impact on my life.

Music was and still is a big part of my life. I grew up listening to everything from country to rap, hip-hop, to opera. During the good and bad times, there is nothing better than a great song or familiar melody. Music made life seem clear when I didn't understand. Music influenced me to keep going when I felt like giving up. I don't know where I would be if it were not for music. I remember fantasizing about being a performer when I was growing up. I even had a rap group and a singing group. To be completely honest I still think about it now from time to time, but everything was not meant for everybody so I decided to put those dreams on hold at least for now. I think I was just fascinated with the whole entertainment industry, especially since my father had a career in television.

I listened to a lot of music growing up, but I also watched just as much television with my sister and brother. When we weren't watching television or listening to music, we were outside playing. We would float around the neighborhood like we ruled the world. One day, we were at an apartment complex getting into trouble and I remember falling in a pool full of water. We walked all the way home with my clothes-soaking wet, but I didn't care. I was just happy to be hanging out with my big brother and sister.

I'm sure my sister and brother have their own version or memories of what happened while we were growing up. I look forward to sitting down with them one day to reminisce over the experiences that we share. We didn't have the best of everything growing up, but we made the best out of what we had. The experience of growing up in a constantly changing environment taught me how to make the best out of any situation. My mentor and good friend once said "your beginning does not have to determine your end" and with that in mind, I have listed the following information in hopes that at least one person finds the strength to keep going even when the road ahead seems unclear and uncertain.

How to make the best out of any situation

1. Pick your battles wisely.

2. Be optimistic.

3. Keep an open mind.

4. Be able to adapt to change.

5. Use what you have to get what you want.

6. Don't sweat the small stuff.

7. Learn how to turn a negative situation into a positive situation.

8. Use your negative experiences to create opportunities for more positive experiences.

9. Go with the flow of things.

10. Learn how to live and let go.

It's important to make the best out of situations when they arise because tomorrow isn't promised and no one wants to live a life that is full of regrets. There will be times when we will be placed in uncompromising situations, but we must learn how to deal with those situations and keep it moving.

Life has a way of throwing a curveball every now and then. In those particular situations, we have to do the best that we can do. No one is perfect and as I previously mentioned, there are things in life that are simply inevitable. Everything happens for a reason. There is a cause and effect for everything that happens in life.

The cause is the reason or motive that something happens. The effect is the result of what happened. Growing up in a constantly changing environment not only taught me how to make the best out of any situation, it also caused me to grow up a little faster than most kids. My parent's worked hard and made a genuine effort to raise me to the best of their ability. I appreciate my parent's effort, despite the animosity that grew between them.

CHAPTER 3

LAZY HANDS MAKE A WOMAN POOR

My mother was not lazy by a long shot; she would work her fingers to the bone if she had to. My mother would work in that plant day in and day out. I don't know how she did it, but she did. My mother worked like a slave slinging car parts. I would listen to her talk about all the politics of working in the plant and all the stress that came with it.

I remember listening to conversations about who was drunk and on drugs, who got hurt, who came and who left. The plant was a miniature soap opera. I couldn't imagine what other people's life was like that worked in the plant, but I knew what life was like for my mother. I also knew that I didn't want to work there no matter what they were paying.

Working in the plant was no fun no matter how you looked at it. I have the upmost respect for anyone that managed to make a career out of it. My mother's health and mental state started to deteriorate while working in that madness, but she had to make a living and that was all she knew how to do, so I really didn't blame her for staying. I admired my mom for being a strong and diligent worker. Those were two of the qualities that I definitely inherited from my mother. These qualities would unfortunately come back to haunt me later on in life.

My mother just wasn't good at balancing her career and family. She would bring her problems home from work and vice versa. She didn't know how to balance her career with her personal life or raising her children. I learned that too much of anything is not good for you, work included. In order to have peace of mind, you must have balance in all aspects of your life. When you spend too much time doing one thing, you better believe that something else is being neglected. Living a balanced life is not always easy and I had to find this out the hard way later on in life.

How to live a balanced life

1. Plan ahead.

2. Don't waste time.

3. Be organized and efficient.

4. Don't over exert yourself.

5. Make time for yourself.

6. Make time for family and friends.

7. Keep your spirit uplifted.

8. Get plenty of rest.

9. Exercise.

10. Eat small nutritious well-balanced meals throughout the day.

Balance is important. My philosophy is that too much of anything can kill you. My quality of life could have been improved tremendously if my mother would have found a way to live a more balanced life. I listed 10 simple steps a person can take to live a more balanced life. It is natural for things to become unbalanced from time to time, but it doesn't take much to get back on track if you are like me or the million other people that manage to fall off. The most important thing is to make a change before things get too out of hand.

As far as my mother is concerned, she never learned how to balance her work and personal life. She tried to live a balanced life but nothing was ever consistent. She went through one bad relationship after another and it was always one problem after the next. She never took time out for herself or off work unless it was heavily mandated by a doctor, otherwise, she would be at work rain, sleet, hail or snow. Since my mother worked so much, my sister and brother had to look after me.

CHAPTER 4

OUT WITH THE OLD IN WITH THE NEW

By the time I was 4 years old, my sister and brother weren't living with us anymore. My sister and brother kept getting into trouble according to my mother, so she decided that they would be better off living with other family members. The house felt somewhat empty without them around. My father came around a little more often. I remember one day in particular, my father came to visit. It must have been close to Christmas because we all went to the toy store. My mother and father told me to pick out a bike, but when I told them which bike I wanted, they told me to pick out something else. I cried and cried until I couldn't cry anymore, but to my surprise, on Christmas day, my bike was waiting for me with training wheels and all. I loved that bike, even though I barely knew how to ride it. I scarred up my legs plenty of times trying to learn.

My mother enrolled me in preschool. I even took piano lessons for a minute. I enjoyed being around other kids. I remember sharing my first kiss coming down the slide. I was caught off guard and don't know where it came from, but I remember feeling special. When I was promoted to kindergarten, my mom had a special gathering for me. I was excited yet nervous about kindergarten, so my mother enrolled me into a private school.

Things eventually started to change around the house again. My grandfather was getting older so my mother had him come live with us. From what I remember, my mother was close to her father, especially since my grandmother died when my mother was just a little girl. Shortly after my grandfather came to live with us, he passed away in his sleep. My mother was never the same again. I don't know if she felt guilty or lost because he was gone. Maybe she felt a little bit of both. My grandfather liked to smoke cigarettes and drink. My mother had no problem contributing to his habits and I'm sure that his bad habits probably contributed to his death.

My mother broke down mentally and started going in and out of the hospital. She eventually pulled herself together again long enough to start dating someone that she had met at work. His name was Tim. Things were good for a short while. Tim treated me like a little princess. My mother and I would get our hair done together every two weeks. I remember the very first time we went to the salon together and I got my very first perm. It hurt like hell but when it was all over, I left looking like a little diva. I also remember having the best birthday party when I was 5 years old. I wore a red dress and my hair hung down my back in Shirley Temple curls. I knew I looked like a princess that day, I had so much fun. I twirled around so much that my nose began to bleed. I will never forget that very special day, as well as all the gifts I received. One of the gifts was a fur coat, which I wore on Easter. I remember watching movies with my mom. One night, we stayed up late watching Purple Rain. I can never forget that night because that was the first time that my mother and I had a real conversation. I remember her telling me to never let a man put his hands on me. Out of all the things she told me, that stuck with me even to this day. My mother had been through a lot and she had some serious issues. I didn't understand until I got older. A lot of it had to do with her work, failed relationships, and raising children on her own, but most of it had to do with my mother's unstable upbringing. My grandmother died when my mother was around 12 years old. My mother had to live with different family members and she had a rough upbringing. She grew up having to fend for herself. It was only natural that my mother would raise us similar to how she was raised. For some children, that type of upbringing might have worked out, but not for me or my siblings. We didn't require much, we just wanted a little of the 3 A's acceptance, affection, and attention. We wanted our mother to accept us despite who our fathers were and what they had done. We wanted her to give us the affection that all children deserve and provide us with the attention that we needed instead of expecting us to fend for ourselves.

Although there were times in my life when things were unstable, I learned to live and let go. I let go of the fact my sister and brother weren't around the house any more. I let go of the fact my grandfather passed and he wouldn't be around to see me grow up. I let go of the fact my mother always worked and our time together was limited. I learned to live and simply let go.

How to live and let go

1. Remember that life is what you make it so change your thinking.

2. Stop worrying and obsessing.

3. Relax, relate, release.

4. Learn how to be patient.

5. Live a purpose driven life.

6. Live a balanced life.

7. Live creatively and productively.

8. Forgive but don't forget.

9. Leave the past behind.

10. Let go and let God.

As a child, it was simple letting go of some of life's unpleasant events, but as we grow and get older, this becomes harder to do. I listed 10 ways in which a person can learn how to live and let go of whatever it is that maybe holding them back or preventing them from moving forward. Learning how to live and let go is a very important part of life. So many of us carry baggage and dead weight from one part of our life to the next and it isn't healthy. Carrying old baggage and dead weight prevents us from living a life of substance and meaning. Everyone has a purpose and that purpose does not consist of carry old baggage, so let it go.

CHAPTER 5

A CHILD IS BORN

A few months after my grandfather died, my mother gave birth to my little brother. I didn't know she was pregnant, but after he was born, and I saw him for the first time, I thought he was undoubtedly the most handsome little boy I had ever seen. People called him Butterball because he was huge. He was always happy except for on the few occasions that I would make him cry.

When my brother came along things changed around the house again. Tim and my mother would argue from time to time. I would cry or start acting out for attention. My mother suffered another mental breakdown. I don't know if it was the joys of motherhood or a build up of everything that she had been through. Whatever it was, it upset her pretty badly because she tried to burn the house down with my little brother and me in it.

I don't remember much about what happened because I have subconsciously tried to suppress or block out those memories and so much has happened over the years, but from what I do remember, the day started out normal. I went outside to play with my friends like I usually did. When I came back in the house later that afternoon, my mom was somehow different. She didn't seem her usual self. She seemed as if something was bothering her. Before I knew it, she had taken me into the basement and started washing my hair. She washed my hair with bleach, laundry detergent, and a few other household products that were near by. Believe it or not that experience didn't hurt nearly as bad as it did compared to when I got my first perm, but it was the scene that took place afterwards that left me somewhat scarred.

I remember her carrying me back upstairs with a towel wrapped around my head. Smoke was coming from everywhere. I heard my little brother crying at the top of his lungs. As soon as my mother put me down, I ran next door to my neighbor's house. People began showing up from everywhere. My dad came, my aunt came, and it was almost like a family reunion despite the circumstances. The police even showed up.

My mother was admitted into a mental facility and I went to go live with my Aunt Ann and Uncle John. They had six children, but the two oldest didn't live in the house. I loved playing with my cousins, but I managed to get myself into trouble. I remember climbing up on the sink and it broke. I placed toothpaste and toilet tissue around the edges in place of the caulk hoping no one would notice. When my Uncle found out about what I had done, he was furious and I got a good old fashion spanking. My cousins and I was always into something. I had a lot of fun but I also got into a lot of trouble. I don't know if that was my way of dealing with all that I had gone through with my mother or my way of simply acting out for attention. I experienced some very tragic events at an early age. Loosing my grandfather and witnessing my mother suffer from a mental break down was devastasting. Dealing with tragedy is not an easy thing to do. It's a very sensitive subject because people handle life's tragic events differently, but there are a few simple things that people can consider when a tragedy occurs. I listed 10 ways in which a person can learn how to deal with tragedy because no one knows when a tragedy will take place and its always better to be safe than sorry. I know this sounds cliché, but as previously stated, if I had known then what I know now; I would be a much different person. Everyone deals with tragedy differently. The information that I provided is a set of general guidelines a person can use, but it is always best to consult a professional. By no means are any of my suggestions meant to be used in place of professional help.

How to deal with tragedy

1. Accept that you cannot change what happened.

2. Learn how the tragedy affects you.

3. Get in touch with yourself.

4. Find the unknown strength within you.

5. Know that it takes time to recover from a tragedy.

6. Talk about your feelings with someone you trust.

7. Find closure.

8. Live and let go.

9. Move forward with a positive mindset.

10. Seek professional help if necessary.

CHAPTER 6

SPARE THE ROD & SPOIL THE CHILD

I love my Aunt more than words can ever express. I would spend the night over her house from time to time, but things were much different living with my Aunt compared to living with my mother. I was only about six years old but I remember feeling as if I was apart of a real family. My Aunt treated me as if I were one of her children. I never felt out of place. My Aunt was always good to me even when I got in trouble. When it was time to pass out punishments, I knew exactly what I was getting in trouble for even if it wasn't my fault. For instance, one of my cousins ate a whole watermelon without permission and tried to hide it by putting the left over watermelon rinds down the toilet. When my Aunt and Uncle found out, we knew we were in for one of those good old fashion spankings, so we prepared for it by stuffing ourselves with toilet paper and several layers of clothes. By the time my Uncle realized what we had done; he couldn't do anything, but sit back and laugh about the whole thing. We never found out who the culprit was but I had a good idea who did it.

My cousins and I were always into something. We skipped school and played in abandoned houses. We got into fights with other kids from the neighborhood if they so much as even looked at us wrong. It was crazy thinking about how much trouble we got into at such an early age. My Aunt and Uncle worked a lot so we spent quite a bit of time by ourselves or at the neighbor's house.

My father dropped by on a few occasions to spend time with me. I enjoyed spending time with him because I was always learning something new or doing something fun. I was proud of my father and happy every time I was in his presence. I didn't like for him to leave, but I had gotten use to it over the years and I learned how to enjoy my time with him while it lasted. Although I learned things with my father, I learned my most valuable lessons living in my aunt's house. She taught me the meaning of family and the importance of being patient.

How to have patience

1. Remember what matters.

2. Make the most out of the present situation.

3. Be reasonable.

4. Slow down.

5. Give yourself a break.

6. Learn how to have self control.

7. Learn how to take control of your own destiny.

8. Do all that you can do then let go and wait.

9. Remind yourself that being patient will increase your happiness & help you live a better life.

10. Remind yourself that things take time.

My Aunt is one of the most patient women I know. I never saw her break a sweat over anything. She accepted me into her home and took me in as one of her own children out of the kindness of her heart. She also displayed a tremendous amount of patience with me when most people would have given up. I listed 10 ways in which a person can become more patient. I hope that I have influenced at least one person to gain a better understanding of the importance of being patient and holding on just a little while longer. Regardless of what you are going through, hold on and be patient because your blessing is coming. There is an old saying that "good things come to those who wait" so with this in mind, be patient and hold on because the best is yet to come.

CHAPTER 7

LEAD US NOT INTO TEMPTATION

Eventually, it was decided that it would be best if I went to live with my father and his wife. I was excited and it gave me an opportunity to spend time with my little sister. My first night in my father's home was good. I remember my stepmother coming home after working at the hospital. She made brownies and gave me some vanilla ice cream. We had the time of our life.

Shortly thereafter, I found out that I had another little sister on the way. I remember anticipating her arrival. I wanted to know how she was going to look and how she was going to act. I was so excited. My other little sister and I stayed at the neighbor's house until my stepmother was discharged from the hospital. When the baby arrived, she was beautiful and such a little sight to see.

When it was time for my stepmother to go back to work, we started going to a babysitter. She would watch us and make sure I got off to school while my father and stepmother were working. I participated in a few extracurricular activities while I was in school. I played both the violin and clarinet at one point. I would help out around the house as much as I could because I was the oldest. My stepmother taught me certain things like how to iron my own clothes and wash dishes. I was naturally mischievous so I still managed to get into trouble from time to time. I would go in my stepmother's nail polish and polish my nails. I would go in my father's change jar for coins. Every time I turned around, I was getting in trouble for something.

My father and stepmother worked different hours so we didn't do much together as a family. My father would take us places. My stepmother would also take us on outings while my dad was at work. I do remember us all being together for the holidays. They were the best because we always dressed up real nice. We would go to my step-grandmother's big beautiful house and eat dinner as a family. We ate everything a person could think of and of course, everything was delicious. We also got the best toys on Christmas. The living room would be filled to capacity with everything a kid could think of, but it wasn't long before things started to change and fall apart just like they did when I was living with my mother.

My father and stepmother would argue with each other from time to time. I knew what some of these arguments were about. The arguments were primarily about other women and I started to feel uncomfortable. I loved my father, but he definitely had his faults and I felt awkward knowing that he was involved with other women while married to my stepmother. I am sure that my stepmother felt as if she was in an awkward position by raising me while he was cheating with other women. I didn't know who to trust or who to talk to so I kept all of my feelings to myself. At this point, I was accustomed to the drama and the arguments. I had seen my mother argue so much that I became immune to the chaos.

I was supposed to spend the night at my Cousin Samantha's house one weekend. After I arrived, we started talking to each other about how things were going since I moved in with my father. My cousin told me that she kept in touch with my mother so I asked her to call her for me. My mother came by immediately after we got off the phone. I was happy to see her and she seemed happy to see me. My cousin agreed to allow me to spend some time with my mother because it had been several months since we last saw each other. We had a lot of catching up to do. I was so excited but I knew a change was coming. I knew something serious was definitely going to happen once my father found out about me leaving with my mother.

How to deal with change

1. Expect the unexpected.

2. Look forward to change.

3. Prepare yourself for change.

4. Don't be afraid of change.

5. Understand the change that is taking place.

6. Understand that change is a part of life.

7. Accept change.

8. Embrace change.

9. Remember that change is inevitable.

10. Create a positive future through change.

As I look back over the situation, I realize that my cousin really stuck her neck out for me and I appreciated what she did. There were many things that went on in my father's home. It was good to get away and spend some time with my mother despite the circumstance that surrounded our visit.

Everyone goes through changes in their life at one point or another. Change is often times inevitable, especially when you have no control over the things that are going on around you. I have learned a lot about change over the years and I listed 10 ways, in which a person can become better at dealing with change. I hope that I have influenced at least one person to adapt to change in a more effective manner.

CHAPTER 8

OBEY THY MOTHER & THY FATHER

My mother was living in an apartment and she had a new boyfriend named Anthony. After I started telling her some of the things that was happening at my father's house, she told me I didn't have to go back and I could live with her. When my father found out, things got real ugly. The police came to my mother's apartment and made me return to live with my father. He had full custody of me and there wasn't much that my mother could do.

After I went back to live with my father and stepmother, things didn't get any better, in fact, they only got worse. I loved my father enormously, but he crossed the line with me. He violated me, as well as my trust. My whole view of him had changed overnight. I did not know what to do or what to say. On one hand, my father meant everything to me. On the other hand, I was confused and torn. I felt guilty and bad about ever going to live with him. The worse things got around the house, the more I realized I couldn't stay there anymore. I had to leave so I went to school, called my mother from the payphone and I told her everything. I pleaded with her to do something. She told me that everything was out of her hands and she couldn't deal with the situation, so I decided to talk to the teacher and principle at my school. Before I knew it, I was explaining what happened over and over again. I was really tired of talking about it. I just wanted to move on and forget the whole thing had ever happened.

From that point on, my life has never been the same. The events and things that took place over these few short years of my life left me permanently scarred. I have tried to suppress many of those old memories, but they still mange to resurface from time to time. I am still dealing with a lot of the pain and guilt, but I don't let it get the best of me. The wounds have healed but the scars are still there.

I listed 10 ways in which a person can learn how to heal past wounds. I hope that I have influenced at least one person to learn the importance of forgiveness. I intentionally left out many details about the things that went on in my father's home because that chapter of my life is closed. I have tried to forgive and get pass that point in my life so that those wounds can heal properly. My mother was given temporary custody of me, but she became overwhelmingly stressed out. She wasn't thrilled about going through a long court case and of course she blamed me for going to live with my father in the first place. As far as she was concerned, everything that happened was my fault. She also had the nerve to tell me that I always put my father before her as if she was trying to say I got what I deserved. This whole experience was very painful for me.

How to heal past wounds

1. Give yourself time to heal.

2. Don't carry past wounds into new experiences.

3. Open up and don't keep feelings bottled up.

4. Talk to some one you trust.

5. Stay encouraged.

6. Challenge yourself to do things different the next time around.

7. Live your life.

8. Let go of old baggage.

9. Find closure.

10. Accept what happened and move forward.

CHAPTER 9

STOP DOING WRONG

By the time I was 9 years old, things started to get even worse. It seemed like I was always doing something wrong. I started rebelling against my mother. A part of me resented her for not being there for me. Another part of me wanted to prove that my life did not revolve around her and I was going to make it in this world with or without her.

When my mother felt like she needed a break or didn't want to be bothered with raising me, she would send me over to Aunt Charlene's house. Charlene wasn't my real aunt but she had known my mother since she was a teenager and she was one of my mother's closest friends.

Aunt Charlene had 3 boys and one girl. She was married and her husband also worked in the automotive industry with my mother. I don't remember too much about Aunt Charlene's two older sons because they were never around but I remember having the time of my life with her two youngest children Tiffany and Percy. Tiffany was about ten years older than me and Percy was about 4 years older than me. Tiffany was like the big sister that I always wanted and Percy was cool to be around. Tiffany would talk to me and help me with all the girl stuff. Percy would undo all her hard work by turning me into a tomboy. We would jump off of things, listen to rap music and he would even let me ride his dirt bike.

Tiffany and Percy were well taken care of. Tiffany was the only girl so it was only natural that she was spoiled rotten. Tiffany was very confident and had the best of everything. She even had her own place and I would spend the night with her from time to time. For her nineteenth birthday, her mom rented her a convertible corvette. Later that night, Tiffany and her friends all went out to celebrate her birthday. It was fun watching her get all dressed up and ready to go out. I secretly wished I was old enough to get dressed up and go with her but I wasn't, so I improvised by listening to the live broadcast that would be playing on the radio from all the hottest clubs on Friday night. I would dance my little heart out, even though I could not dance one bit.

The next day, when Tiffany would wake up, I would listen to her talk about everything that happened. I could just imagine all the fun she had hanging out at the club with all of her friends. I never saw her go out alone. She always had a date. Each one of them would be dressed to kill. I'm sure that all eyes were on her and her friends when they stepped in the nightclub.

Styles came and went as trends changed. At 9 years old, I knew a lot about fashion and had a great sense of style, but I lacked confidence. I'm not sure if I lacked confidence because of the things that I went through as a child or from the fact that no one taught me what being confident meant. I didn't understand that confidence is not about what you wear, it is how you wear it. I learned the importance of confidence and how far it can get you later on in life. When you lack confidence, people can usually sense it. When you are confident, you have the ability to achieve anything you want in life as long as you are willing to work for it. Obtaining the things that you want in life requires planning and setting goals. When you set realistic goals and have confidence, the world is at your fingertips, you just have to reach out and grab it.

When you are confident and believe in yourself, others can tell and they will believe in you also. I realize that confidence is not solely based on what you have or what you wear. I also realize that confidence does not come overnight and there are many factors that contribute to a person's level of confidence, but being confident is a huge part of setting and achieving goals. I listed 10 ways in which a person can set and achieve goals because I feel that it is vital to have goals and to know how to achieve them. I hope that I have influenced at least one person to have confidence, set higher goals, and live a more fulfilled life.

How to set goals and achieve your goals

1. Be confident.

2. Believe in yourself.

3. Know what you want.

4. Figure out what it takes to get what you want.

5. Set goals.

6. Set goals over a realistic time frame.

7. Write your goals down.

8. Discuss your goals.

9. Review your goals frequently.

10. Check your progress...get ahead, don't fall behind.

CHAPTER 10

SHE WHO GUARDS HER LIPS GUARDS HER LIFE

At the end of summer, I went back to go live with my mother. Things weren't any different. She had her opinion and I had mine, but I just kept my opinion to myself. My mother had high expectations of me but she couldn't understand that I required acceptance, affection, and attention. All the fun and fashionable things that we used to do together was a thing of the past. We didn't get our hair done together anymore and most of my clothes came from the second hand store.

I couldn't win for losing. I wasn't even going to try. I hadn't done anything wrong and I definitely didn't plan on doing anything wrong, but you couldn't tell my mother that because when something went wrong, it was always my fault. I got tired of being blamed for everything. It was like she was waiting for an excuse to ship me off somewhere like she did my other siblings. I stayed to myself and just shut down so she had me admitted into a mental hospital. She concocted an elaborate story to have me admitted. She said "I was mentally traumatized and I refused to listen to her." The way I saw it was simple, why should I listen to her when she was always fussing and yelling about the same old thing.

I didn't like the mental hospital but it beat having someone scream at you all day. It was almost like a vacation when I blocked out the barbed wire fences and the fools being carried away in straitjackets because they didn't know how to act or follow directions. Most of the patients that were in the facility with me were on medication and it never seemed to kick in because they were always being reprimanded. I made the mistake of losing my temper one time when I didn't get what I wanted and I vowed never to make that mistake again. I had forgotten where I was and I didn't like being reminded by staff. There was nothing worse than smelly, overweight grown women trying to restrain a 9-year-old little girl. From that point on, I stayed out of trouble and remained self disciplined. I don't know exactly how long I was there, but it didn't take me long to get out. I went during the middle of the summer and I got out right on time to start a new school that same year.

I didn't understand why my mother did some of the things she did and I desperately wanted things to be different between us. I loved my mother and I understood that being a parent was not an easy job. Regardless of the trials and tribulations that my mother and I went through, I always tried to maintain a certain level of respect for her. I looked forward to going home with my mom and starting my new school.

Even though I knew I didn't belong in the mental hospital, I learned some very valuable life lessons from that experience. One of the most valuable lessons that I learned was how to be self disciplined. I have listed 10 ways in which a person can become self-disciplined because it is an important aspect of life. I hope that my testimony has influenced at least one person to live a more disciplined life.

How to be self disciplined

1. Learn how to have self-control.

2. Learn how to set goals.

3. Learn how to live a purpose driven life.

4. Learn how to manage your time wisely.

5. Don't procrastinate.

6. Challenge yourself.

7. Plan ahead.

8. Be organized.

9. Be efficient.

10. Be consistent.

Getting adjusted to everything was harder than I thought it would be because we moved three times in one year. We moved from one apartment building to another. Moving wasn't that bad because the old apartment building was infested with roaches. In addition to the building being infested with roaches, it was also a criminal's playground. One of my mother's friends was found dead in their apartment. Decomposing maggots were seen everywhere and the foul odor had the apartment building smelling for days.

The next apartment we moved to wasn't located too far from our old apartment and it was very nice. I got my first job passing out sales papers and flyers around the apartment complex. We were eventually evicted when my mother refused to pay rent after a shelving unit fell down on me. Being evicted was one of the most embarrassing things that ever happened to me because everything we owned was put out in the alley and trash.

The next place we moved to was a two family flat. We stayed upstairs and my cousin Tiffany stayed downstairs. I had many friends and of course, I got into a lot of trouble. We stayed there for years. I really enjoyed living there, although we didn't live in the best neighborhood and we stayed quite a distance from my school.

CHAPTER 11

THIEVES AMONG US

School was all right, although I was a little intimidated at first because I felt like all the kids were smarter than me and they came from better families. I got into a fight with a girl because she kept talking about me in a derogatory manner. We were going at it like cats and dogs, but when everything was said and done, we were both suspended. When I came back to school, no one messed with me and I even made a few friends. I tried my hardest to stay out of trouble until me and my new friends decided to steal a few things from a store one day. We would pass the store every day on our way to the bus stop going home from school.

I didn't like stealing because I knew that it was wrong. I also knew the consequences if I were to ever get caught. My mother would yell at me from here to eternity and that was the last thing I wanted her to do. I wouldn't dare give her something else to yell at me about. I could hear her voice now, talking about me the same way she would talk about my older sister and brother. I never had money and that day was no different. My mother would give me just enough money to catch the bus to and from school. The way I saw the situation seemed simple back then but now that I look back, I don't know what the hell I was thinking. I knew better.

My friends filled me in on the game plan and I hesitatingly said "ok," even though things didn't feel right. It was about four of us so we decided to split up so we wouldn't look obvious. We walked around to see what we could steal. The more and more I tried to figure out what I was going to take, the more and more I began to hear my mother's voice. I started panicking because I couldn't steal anything to big or I might get caught. If I was going to steal anything at all, it had to be worth it, so I thought long and hard while my friends were busy stuffing their pockets.

Unfortunately, while I was trying to figure out what to steal, my friends got caught. My loud mouth self should have kept on moving, but I didn't want to leave my friends and then have to face them in school, so I started asking questions. The security guard took a good look at me and said, "Are you with these girls?" I said, "Yes!" like I was somebody important, so he took me too. He escorted us to the basement of the store into a creepy back room and said, "Empty your pockets." I had nothing to empty but my friends on the other hand had a pocket full of crap. They had all kinds of candy, makeup, nail polish, and toys.

The police arrived shortly after that and we were given a long talk. The store didn't press charges against my friends. We were only 11 years old. It was too late for us to go home by ourselves so the police said they would make sure we got home safely. After we left the store, the police officers decided to take a detour to the police headquarters. I was confused and baffled because I thought we were going straight home. When we arrived at the police station, we were fingerprinted and escorted through the jail. The police officers decided to use a couple of scare tactics to make sure we wouldn't end up in trouble again. When they finally did take me home, my mother was furious and mad as hell just like I knew she would be. The police explained what happened but she didn't care. I didn't even bother trying to explain why I was hanging with my friends instead of coming straight home or how I got caught. I just went to bed hoping for the day to come when I could take care of myself so I didn't have to live in my mother's household.

The next day, report cards were sent home, which only made matters worse. I had a B, a D, and the rest were all C's. I thought I did pretty well, especially since I had to wake myself up, get dressed on my own, and head off to school on my own every morning, but my mother didn't see it that way.

Unfortunately, things aren't always the way they seem and although my mother thought she was raising me the best way she could, I thought she could do a much better job at being a parent and so did the juvenile court system because that is exactly where I eventually ended up.

My mother was no stranger to the court system because my older brother and sister were both court wards. My mother had a cycle that she had no interest in breaking. My mother would have children and by the time she felt they were old enough to do for themselves, she would abandon them. This went on for many years.

There is no way to describe every emotion, event, obstacle, or pain that I have experienced. I can't compare my life to a box of chocolates, if anything, I would say it was more like a bag of trail mix because as nutty as my mother was, you never knew what you were going to get. One minute she would be up, the next minute she would be down. One minute she would be happy, the next minute she would be sad. I never knew how to act around my mother because she was capable of snapping at anytime.

My mother tried to have me admitted into another mental hospital. When the hospital refused to admit me because they didn't find anything wrong with me, she flipped out. They suggested that she was the one with the mental problem and I should be placed with protective services. I was immediately removed from my mother's home and taken to a shelter.

I was scared and didn't know what to expect but certain things became more important to me at that point. School was one of those things. I wanted be a better student, a better person all together. I was starting to get tired of going through changes. I just wanted someone to be proud of me. I remember telling myself that once I made it past this situation, I was going to focus on my schoolwork and stay out of trouble. I knew that my grades weren't going to improve overnight, but I knew that my confidence could.

I listed 10 ways in which a person can become a better student. I hope that my testimony has influenced at least one person to take advantage of learning and get the best education possible. As I look back at the situation and think about the things that I did wrong, I find myself being grateful for the experience because I learned a very valuable lesson and things could have been much worse. Social services tried to make things as easy as possible on me so they put me in a shelter that was close to my home and they also allowed me to remain at my same school.

How to be a good student

1. Be ambitious.

2. Be committed to learning.

3. Be enthusiastic about learning.

4. Be a good listener.

5. Be open-minded.

6. Be organized.

7. Be respectful.

8. Be self-disciplined.

9. Be self-motivated.

10. Be self-reliant.

CHAPTER 12

FREE YOURSELF

It was the middle of the night when I arrived and I didn't know what to expect. When morning came, I woke up and looked around. I was nervous because most of the girls looked older than me. I took a long shower, got dressed, ate breakfast, and spent the rest of the day talking to counselors and staff. I was only there about a month or two, but I saw a lot happen. I got along with everyone for the most part. I did get into a fight and couple of arguments but nothing major. When it was time for me to leave the shelter, I started visiting different foster parents.

Eventually, I was placed with a family. My foster mother worked for the bank and she had a nice house. She coached girls' basketball for a private school and took care of her son and his daughter. Her son lived in the basement when he wasn't over his girlfriend's house. His daughter was a little bit younger than me, but we got along pretty well. I liked her, but she was just spoiled as hell and she always had to have her way. She reminded me somewhat of myself believe it or not.

From what I remember her telling me, her mother used to be on crack. I couldn't imagine what that was like for her but I know that it could not have been any worse than what I was going through with my mother.

Crack was a huge epidemic during the 80's and 90's. I didn't know anyone that used crack but I knew plenty of people that sold it. I grew up watching what crack did to people and I knew it wasn't for me. I would see plenty of public service announcements that described what drugs would do to people that used them. I heard "Just Say No To Drugs" so much that I wondered how could anyone possibly say yes. In addition to all the public service announcements every time I turned around, I was hearing a rap about drugs. One rap happened to be called "Your Mama On Crack Rock." My friends and I thought it was the funniest thing. Although I went to one of the best schools in Detroit, it was located right next door to a rundown apartment building. I remember looking outside my classroom window seeing women prostituting themselves for a quick fix. It was wild. I remember seeing an argument between a drug dealer and prostitute. The whole thing was crazy and reminded me of the movie "New Jack City." I admit, I was somewhat intrigued by my surroundings. I wondered what would lead people to live that type of lifestyle. I didn't understand how women could sell themselves for money or drugs. I didn't understand how people could get so caught up in the world that they could resort to something so minute. Sometimes my friends and I would tease the drug addicts when we were out on the playground. I don't know what I was thinking because it didn't dawn on me until it was almost time to leave school that I would have to pass the same people on my way home. As funny as it sounds, I started praying everyday on my way to and from school. I learned about the power of prayer and building my faith when I was back at the shelter, so prayer was nothing new to me. If it were not for prayer, I don't know where I would be. As I mentioned earlier, I don't get too much off into religion, but I believe in GOD and I know that there is a higher power that sustains us all. We live in a world of limitless possibilities. All that we are required to do is have faith.

I learned the power of prayer and the importance of having faith at an early age. I listed 10 ways in which a person can build their faith. I hope that my testimony influences at least one person to be lead by the power of GOD and understand the importance of having faith. Prayer changes things, I know first-hand. I enjoyed living with my foster family but I also prayed to be back with my own family. I felt like an outsider while I was living in foster care. I was so use to changes that I never felt comfortable being in one place for too long.

How to build your faith

1. Believe
2. Meditate
3. Pray
4. Praise
5. Reflect
6. Refocus
7. Renew
8. Repent
9. Tithe
10. Worship

CHAPTER 13

LOVE AT FIRST SIGHT

I lived with my foster family for several months until the court awarded custody of me back to my Aunt and Uncle. I was happy to be back in a familiar place. I remember having so much fun with my cousins. One of my cousins would let me wear all of her clothes. I was wearing Guess, Nautica, Polo, Tommy Hilfiger, K-Swiss, Nikes, and a whole bunch of other name brand clothes. We would do each other's hair in the best hairstyles. Any hairstyle that we saw, I would duplicate it on my cousin then teach her how to do my hair the exact same way. We would also sit back for hours and reminisce over all the trouble we used to get into. We were bad as hell, especially back when I first lived with them. We still managed to get into trouble every now and again, but it was mostly over keeping the house clean and talking on the phone with boys. I was only 13 years old when I began to seriously think about boys.

The first time that I knew I was bitten by the love bug was when my cousins and I were at a carnival. I met this boy that seemed to appear from out of nowhere. He was tall, dark, and handsome. He was dressed nice and somewhat preppy. He had good hair and the most charming smile. I guess he noticed me around the same time I noticed him because we just stared at each other for a moment. When we finally stopped staring at each other, he approached me and asked me my name. I was in shock so I just stood there for a moment because I couldn't think straight. I blurted out Erica, which was my middle name. He then told me his name was Marlon. We spent the rest of the day at the carnival together. When the carnival ended, he walked me and my cousins back to our house. We exchanged phone numbers and he called me later that night.

Marlon was 16 and I was only 13. He was in high school and I was in middle school. He worked and I didn't. He had a car and I didn't. The only thing we had in common was our attraction to one another. He was everything that I would want in a boyfriend because he looked good and he was smart. He went to Cass Tech, one of the best high schools in Detroit, which happened to be right down the street from Burton International where I attended middle school. We talked a lot on the phone and became good friends. We would talk about everything but our relationship didn't go too far because I was too young for him and shortly after we met, I was on the move again. Nevertheless, we remained good friends.

As soon as my mother found out I was living with my Aunt, she wanted me back. She picked me up from my Aunt and Uncle's home while they were at work. She took me over one of her friend's house. They enrolled me into a new school. My mother hadn't changed, she was still her same old crazy self, so things didn't work out and I ended up in a group home. I could have went back to stay with my Aunt and Uncle but I was too ashamed to go back. I felt a little guilty about leaving my Aunt and Uncle after everything they went through to get me. Although I know they loved me unconditionally, I was afraid of how they would treat me if I went back. My mother blamed me for wanting to live with my father and for that reason; I assumed that my Aunt and Uncle might blame me for going with my mother. The whole thing reminded me of the situation that took place with my father. The only difference was that in that situation, I had valid reasons for not wanting to go back and live in my father's house. It was not easy leaving my family and friends behind to go live in a group home.

I didn't know a whole lot about friendship or what it meant to be a good friend. I moved around so much that I never had a chance to get close to anyone except Marlon. The bond that I shared with my cousins was stronger than the bond that I had with my own brothers and sisters. Healthy friendships are important so I listed 10 ways in which a person can be a good friend or maintain the friendships that they already have.

How to be a good friend

1. Be considerate!
2. Be courteous!
3. Be a cheerful giver!
4. Be honest!
5. Be humble & grateful!
6. Be kind!
7. Be positive!
8. Be respectful!
9. Be realistic about your expectations of others!
10. Be straightforward!

CHAPTER 14

AN EYE FOR AN EYE

About a month later, I was placed with another foster parent. She worked at the court for the Sheriff's Department. She had a son but he lived at a boarding school. She was engaged to be married. She worked a lot and when she wasn't working, she was with her fiancée. She was barely around so I managed to get myself into trouble while living in her house. I got into a fight one day coming home from school and ended up suspended. After that little episode, I didn't get into trouble for awhile until I started skipping school. My friends introduced me to a couple of boys from the neighborhood. We would hang out and skip school sometimes but that was it. They were into gangs and I wasn't trying to get caught up in that foolishness. I was still crazy about Marlon, but we lived on opposite sides of town so I rarely got the chance to see him. I did eventually get caught skipping school and my foster mother was fed up. It was getting closer to her wedding day and she had a lot to deal with so she recommended that I be placed somewhere else.

Shortly after, I was placed with my third foster mother. When I first arrived, I didn't know what to expect because the home was right around the corner from my father's house. She had a son that lived with her also. He had recently graduated from college and was engaged to be married in a couple of months to his college sweetheart that lived in California. My foster mother was a little bit older, she didn't work and she always had time for me so I began to really enjoy living with her. I learned a lot about being a young lady and we did a lot of things together on the weekend. We would go to the mall, the movies, and out to eat every Saturday.

Living with my new foster mother brought back a lot of old memories from when I lived with my father because her house was so close to his. I knew that he and my stepmother were divorced. I wondered how he was doing but I wasn't ready to talk to him. I wondered how my Aunt and Uncle were doing as well because I wasn't living that far from them either but I never tried to call. I was too busy focusing on school and adjusting to my new foster home. In only a couple of months, it was time for me to graduate from junior high school. I had the time of my life preparing for my junior prom. I tried on so many different outfits. Eventually, we found the perfect one. It was a one-piece ivory outfit with spaghetti straps. We picked out a bracelet, necklace, a set of earrings, and a pair of ivory colored shoes to match. When the day finally arrived, everything was almost perfect. The only thing that was missing was my date. I had not asked anyone to take me because there was only one person that I would want to take me and that was Marlon, but I hadn't spoken to him in months so I decided to go by myself. I had a good time and said goodbye to most of my friends because most of us were going to separate high schools.

The summer started great. I got a new foster sister. My foster brother was getting married in a couple days so my foster mother flew us out to California to be at the wedding. California was very exciting. This was the very first time that I had ever been outside of Detroit. To top it off, when the wedding was over and we had seen as much of California as we could see, we drove to Las Vegas and stayed at the Circus Hotel and Casino. This was the most fun that I had ever had.

When we returned home, I started working for the summer youth program. It was my first real job and I was excited. I was paid every week, which was right on time because I enjoyed spending money. I would go shopping every Saturday just like we always did, except this time; I was spending my own money. My summer job was quickly coming to an end so I started filling out job applications while I was shopping at the mall. By the time school started, I had a completely new wardrobe. I managed to talk my foster mother into letting me go to the high school that was close to my old middle school, even though it was far from where we lived. By the time school started, Marlon and I were talking more frequently. He was a senior and I was a freshman. We didn't go to the same high school but we did see each other a lot more.

I met many new friends in high school and remained close to some of my old friends from middle school. I still managed to get in trouble every now and then. I was arrested and held at the police precinct when a bus driver tried to close the door on me while I was getting on the bus. I threw a plastic juice bottle at him when he tried to close the door on my leg. I didn't do it on purpose and I really don't know what came over me. I probably should have waited for the next bus, but for some strange reason, I thought about Rosa Parks and figured I had a right to be on the bus. I wasn't prosecuted for throwing the bottle and the bus driver was transferred to another route.

The school year was almost over when I was walking towards that very same bus stop with a group of my friends. I got the strangest feeling. I felt like someone was watching me. When I turned around and looked, I didn't see anyone out of the ordinary; it was the same group of teenagers that I would see everyday hanging out waiting for the bus. When the bus finally arrived I proceeded by boarding the bus and I went straight to the back where I always sat. That is when I noticed David starring at me. We immediately started smiling at each other and it was the weirdest feeling in the world. We would see each other around school and at the bus stop. I don't know if it was my outfit or the way I fixed my hair, but he was attracted to me. I didn't know it at first but I was attracted to him too. He had to be about six feet tall with the whitest teeth that I had ever seen. He was wearing a white Guess t-shirt with black writing on it, black Guess jeans and a pair of Hi-techs.

We exchanged phone numbers but I didn't call him and he didn't call me until a few weeks later. The first time he called, he caught me completely off guard. I didn't think he was going to call me, but when he did, we stayed on the phone for almost an hour. He asked me so many questions and I enjoyed answering them all. I asked him a few questions too, like where he lived, who he stayed with, how old was he, and what grade he was in. He said that he was living with his sister. They had recently moved from one place to another. He had just turned 16 years old and he was in the tenth grade. He also told me that this was his first year at Cody High School because he went to Cass Tech his freshman year. I was impressed until he said he got kicked out for fighting.

The next time he called, we talked for over an hour. After that, he started calling me every day. I didn't notice him at school that much anymore and when I asked him about it, he really didn't explain. He asked me to meet up with him and I gladly accepted. We met at a shopping plaza and hung out for hours. We saw a lot of each other. If we weren't at the shopping plaza we were at his sister's house. I was really starting to like him and then he finally told me. He told me that he was on the run for murder. I was scared at first. I didn't know what to think but for some reason, I still liked him. He explained to me that he shot his sister's boyfriend and he was going to turn himself in. I was stunned and my heart sunk.

I returned home later that day and I didn't say a word to anyone. Time started passing and I hadn't heard from him so I occupied my time with 2 jobs. My first job was working for the summer youth program, which I enjoyed because it was my second time working for the program. My second job was working at a flower shop. There wasn't much for me to do but work. I didn't associate with many of my friends outside of school. Marlon left to start a summer program at the University of Michigan and I still had not heard from David.

Then one day he called from jail. David had someone call me on the three-way. We talked for several minutes and then he asked me for my address. He said that he missed being around me, he thought about me all the time, and he was going to write me as much as he could. A few days later, his letters started arriving in the mail.

July 12, 1995

Dear Marlena

What's up? What have you been up to? I hope that you have been doing ok! As for me, I've just been chilling like the G that I am, staying sucker free and out of trouble. Marlena, I want you to know that I want to be with you when I get out of here. I want to spend the rest of my life with you. I couldn't let you know how I felt because I had too much on my mind. I was on the run and around too many people. The day will come when we will be together. When that day comes I will do everything that a man should do for his woman. I'm going to protect you, take care of you, hold you and love you in more ways than one. Trust me I'm going to be all the man you will ever need and desire. I hope that you stay true to me by not messing with any guys. I'll be writing you back soon and I hope that you'll be doing the same.

David

David's trial started July 31, 2005 and I was there for every minute of it. I would catch the bus to the courthouse faithfully. I sat through every detail. I knew how the murder took place and what David was thinking when he pulled the trigger. He let his temper get the best of him. His mother had passed and his sisters were all that he felt he had. David was a good student. He got into trouble a few times but it was nothing major. He was really a good person but the jury didn't see it that way. When the trial was over, David was found guilty of 2nd degree murder and sentenced to a minimum of 12 years in prison. We talked on the phone as much as possible and we continued to write each other every day.

Dear Marlena

What's up Baby? I know that I just wrote you but I think of you constantly. Right now I am listening to the radio and that is what brought you to my attention. "You Are Not Alone." By Michael Jackson came on and I just started thinking of you. That's exactly what I want you to know. That through all of this you are not alone because I am here for you. And although we are far apart, you are always in my heart. I think of all the dreams I know we share and about the days when they will be reality. I think of how it would be to make love to you every day, about the children we are going to have and the beautiful life that follows. I think about these things everyday knowing that only a short time in our long lives separates us from being together. So look forward to each new day because each day is a prosperous and brighter step towards the rainbow. This is where you will find all of the treasures and dreams that you have been so patiently looking forward to. During the times when I have needed you, you have been there for me. And during the times you will need me I will be there for you. Remember this always.

Love,

David

I really cared about David I didn't think about any other boys including Marlon. I looked forward to our future together because it gave me hope and something to look forward to. At the beginning of my tenth grade year, my foster mother enrolled me into Martin Luther King High School. The school was a little bit closer to the house and I was glad because it was much better compared to Cody, my old high school. Cody had too many bad memories for me. I never told my foster mother about David but his sister came by to see me one day. She had another girl in the car with her that I hadn't seen before. We talked to each other and she asked me questions about my relationship with David. I thought she was one of his family members at first but he had never mentioned her. Eventually, she explained who she was. Her name was Melissa and she turned out to be the mother of David's child. Felecia and I started talking to each other over the phone and comparing the letters, that David had written us. Most of them were different but we did find a couple that were exactly the same.

When David found out, he was furious and he didn't want me talking to her but I didn't care because I was hurt and I wanted closure. I stopped writing him and I didn't accept anymore of his phone calls. We didn't speak to each other for a while but eventually, he wrote me a letter telling me his side of the story.

November 20, 1995

Dear Marlena

How have you been doing? I hope fine. If you've been wondering about me, I'm doing alright. I've just been taking it day by day as usual. I know this letter is unexpected and maybe not wanted. I can understand why if that is the way you feel but I'm writing this letter to, in a sense put those feelings behind. I apologize for all of the trouble that I put you through with all of my lies. All of my statements were not lies but I apologize for anything that I have done to hurt you. This letter is not to try and get you back or anything like that. I just want to let bygones be bygones and let you know that this was all one big misunderstanding. Please know and understand that none of what happened was planned or set up. I just got mixed up. I really don't have to explain or feel I have to; I just want to because it seems necessary. Melissa and I have conversations about the situation and I still don't think she understands this is not all my fault, she's to blame too. You and I started kicking it when I was on the run. Felecia and I weren't on good terms. We were on such bad terms that we never had a conversation without arguing and further more there was confusion as to who's baby Lil Dee was because she was out there doing what she wanted to do. So when me and you started kicking it Melissa was not in the picture. We just recently started back talking for the sake of our son. I couldn't explain that to you because I had feelings for you. I hope you understand that I am not a bad person and I was not trying to play you. It was just a misunderstanding. I thank you for all the things you have given me such as your patience, your company, your comfort and your love when I needed it the most. Well I'm about to go right now. So you keep cool and stay sweet. You don't have to write me back, if you don't want to. AS a matter of fact, I would prefer that you don't so it won't cause any confusion between Felecia and me.

David

I was still hurt but I had to move on with my life and leave it at that. I cut off all communication with him and got another job. This time I was working at the mall. I still worked at the flower shop every now and then when it didn't conflict with my school schedule. I really enjoyed working at the mall because I could shop on my lunch break. I would meet many boys, but I had a hard time trusting them after what David did and it took a while before I found myself interested in anyone else. I met a couple of guys, but it seemed that all they wanted was one thing and I didn't like any of them well enough to give it to them.

Although my relationship with David started out the wrong way, I knew that I cared for him. I wished that things could be different between us because at that point, in time, I couldn't see myself being with anyone else, but I eventually learned to accept the fact that I had to move on. I didn't have anyone to talk to about dating or relationships so I listed 10 ways in which a person should start a relationship because having a solid relationship that is built on a strong foundation is important.

How to start a relationship

1. Close out all past relationships with a good understanding.
2. Be honest and upfront with each other.
3. Have an agreement to be exclusive if that is what both people choose to do.
4. Have an understanding about the relationship.
5. Be consistent.
6. Be a person of your word.
7. Be able to manage and divide your time between school/work, family, friends and your significant other.
8. Spend time with each other on a regular basis.
9. Introduce each other to family and friends.
10. Never lose your identity in a relationship.

CHAPTER 15

AN HONEST ANSWER

Just when I found myself feeling vulnerable, tragedy struck. I was getting my nails done on Christmas Eve. I had just got off work and my foster mother was on her way to a Christmas Eve party, so I decided to call one of the boys I met at the mall. We had talked on the phone several times and he seemed ok so I decided to ask him for a ride home. When he arrived, he was in the car with two other boys and he wasn't the one driving. I started to tell him that was alright and I didn't need a ride anymore but I got into the car anyway. We sat in the back seat and talked to each other for a minute.

Everything was ok at first until the driver decided to make a stop. We weren't that far from my house and I didn't know what was going on. He pulled up to an apartment building and we all got out. We went into the apartment and I politely stood by the door. We didn't stay too long because I guess they could tell that whatever they were trying to sell, I wasn't buying it. They stood around talking for a few more minutes to some people that were already in the apartment when we arrived. I was relieved when we finally left and got back in the car. I thought everything was going to be all right until one of the other passengers started questioning me and talking mess. He apparently had an attitude because I wasn't paying his boy enough attention but I didn't think that was any of his concern. I tried to remain calm and quiet but then he reached back, snatched my herringbone necklace off my neck so we started fighting. His boys tried to stop him, but he wasn't having it and neither was I. They ended up pulling over and putting me out.

I was devastated and scared out of my mind. I hated myself for being so stupid but I guess I got what I deserved at the time. I decided to walk home and I cried most of the way there. When I finally made it, no one was home. I started getting ready for bed when the phone rang. It happened to be the guy from the mall trying to apologize for what happened. I listened for a minute then I started cussing him out. I said every curse word that I could think of before I hung up the phone.

A couple minutes later, the phone rang again and I thought to myself, *I know this boy can't be that dumb*. I picked up the phone and was ready to go off again until the voice on the other end said "Hello." To my surprise, it was Marlon; he was home from college on Christmas break. He asked if he could come by and pick me up. I told him yes even though I didn't feel like leaving, especially after what just happened, but I really wanted to see him and I wasn't allowed to have male company inside my foster mother's house. I wasn't going to take any chances by trying to sneak him in so I got dressed. Not even 30 minutes later, I was out the door. I didn't tell him about anything that happened that day or anything about David because I was too excited to see him and I didn't know how he would react. We went to his mother's house and hung out until I was ready to go home.

Everything was ok until he said he had something to tell me. I thought to myself *"What could it be?"* I asked him *"Is it good or bad?"* He hesitated before he answered then he said "It depends on how you look at it." I asked him not tell me until after he dropped me back off at home because I didn't want to ruin the rest of my Christmas Eve. I made it home before my foster mother so everything worked out well. Eventually, he told me what he had to tell me and I didn't like it one bit. He said he had a son. He started trying to explain how it all happened but I really didn't want to listen. Based on what he told me, he had sex with a girl a few times before he left for college. They weren't in a relationship or anything like that, she was just real loose. He knew her for a while and she already had a child so when she got pregnant she didn't tell anyone until she delivered the baby. When the baby was born, he looked so much like Marlon that she decided to call him and tell him. He went to the hospital. When he saw the baby, he knew it was his. He said he was going to take the baby back to school with him because he didn't want her raising his son. We talked for about an hour and I told him how I felt about him and the entire situation. Regardless of him having a child by someone else, I was still going to be there for him. I always hoped that there would be something more between us. I was very hurt and I let it all come out. He explained how he felt about me as best as possible.

After he was done explaining, I felt a little bit better about the whole situation. I knew he cared about me and that was all that mattered to me so I let the situation go and I put it to the back of my mind. When he went back to school, I wrote him a couple of letters and I told him to write me. In one particular letter, I asked him to seriously think about us being together and I was going to give him until the end of the month for an answer. I suspected that we would never be in a real relationship and my suspicions were confirmed. I received his letter a few days later. I couldn't do anything but respect his decision and move forward.

1/20/96

Dear Marlena

Well I finally did it. I wrote you a letter I didn't tell you because I wanted it to be a surprise. There is only 10 more days until I give you an answer to your question. I'm still not absolutely sure. I am kind of scared to give you an answer because I know whatever I say, yes or no, will change our friendship a lot. If I were to say yes it would mean that sooner or later I would have to be in a serious and faithful relationship with you. If I say no then I might lose a very good friend. I know that you would say that I wouldn't lose but sooner or later I know that you will get tired of me and move on. After all, you are right you can't wait for me forever and you should not have to. I'm just scared of our age difference and I don't think I'm ready for a serious relationship. The last thing that I want to do is hurt you, but it seems like no matter what I choose that is what is going to happen. That is why it is so hard for me to decide and why I am taking so long to decide. Well I have to go but write me back or call me so we can talk about what we should do.

Marlon

Ending a relationship was just as complicated as trying to start one. I had enough confusion going on in my life so I didn't need boys complicating my situation. Ultimately, I knew I wanted to finish school, get married and have children. I longed to have a family like my Aunt and Uncle had. Although it seemed as if neither David nor Marlon were the ones for me, I learned two very valuable lessons on how to start a relationship and how to end one. I listed 10 ways in which a person should end a relationship in hopes that at least one person will be spared the heartbreak and agony of being dumped when they didn't see it coming.

How to end a relationship

1. Don't play games.

2. Know when you want to walk away from the relationship.

3. Make sure you want the relationship to end.

4. Don't make your decisions to end the relationship out of anger.

5. Spend some time apart before abruptly ending the relationship.

6. Don't be confrontational or argumentative.

7. End things respectfully and in a tactful manner.

8. Establish non-negotiable boundaries and stick to them.

9. Don't try to remain friends.

10. Remember the grass always seems greener on the other side.

CHAPTER 16

GOOD UNDERSTANDING WINS FAVOR

After Marlon's letter I really started getting into trouble and staying out late. My foster mother tried to talk to me but I didn't want to listen. When I finally realized I was beside myself it was too late. Things were good while they lasted but I guess nothing lasts forever. Eventually, I ended back in another group home and that was the last place that I wanted to be. That was the first foster home that I allowed myself to be attached to and I was really going to miss living there. I guess that is why from that point on, I never let my guard down and I continued to do what I wanted to do. I didn't like my new group home for some reason, but I wasn't crazy about any of the other ones either. The girls seemed to be different. Most of them stayed doped up on medication. All that I could say was I'm glad I didn't have to be put on medication. I had a phobia of taking medication after seeing what it did to my mother.

The only thing I enjoyed about being in this group home was learning how to play spades and watching music videos. Other than that, I was at school, at work, or on the phone with a boy named Eric that I had met while I was at work. Eric was 19 and I knew he was a thug. I liked his appearance and his bad boy personality, but there was a strange aura that surrounded him. He came up to my job a few times. I even skipped school one time to see him for a couple of hours. I told him to pick me up at a McDonalds off Woodward Avenue. When he pulled up, he was in a black Yukon. He was smelling good and looking just as good. He had on a Pelle Pelle Jacket, a black hooded sweatshirt, Girbaud Jeans, and a pair of Timberlands. We got something to eat, went to his house and I met his mother. I stayed with him for about an hour, then we drove to the mall where I worked. We walked around and hung out before it was time for me to start work.

When I wasn't working and had to be at the group home, there were several occasions when I would just stay in my room or just keep to myself. My roommate was all right, at first. She was only 14 years old and she was pregnant with her second child. We got into an argument one day because she was picking on a girl from another room. I tried taking up for the girl, but she started acting as if she wanted to fight me. I laughed because she was pregnant and she was so little. I would have ripped her into pieces.

Another girl jumped in and started mouthing off, but I just continued laughing because I knew they were just jealous of me. Things quickly started to escalate when I didn't back down, so staff came in and broke it up.

The next day when I got home from work, I noticed that someone had broken into my closet and stole a bunch of my stuff. There was not much that I could do because my roommate and the other girl had run away. They would come up to the mall where I worked but I guess they didn't know that was the wrong thing to do because I told security and had them arrested.

After that little episode, I never saw them again. I really disliked this group home after all of that happened. I started staying away from it as much as possible. I enrolled myself into driver's education when I wasn't working so I could learn how to drive and have something else to do. A few weeks later, I passed and had a driving permit.

Living in group homes was no fun and after my social worker found out everything that was going on in that group home, she moved me to another one. This group home was definitely a lot better than any of the other ones that I was in before. It certainly looked a lot better than the previous ones. The main library, Art Institute, and Science Center were within walking distance and the group home was located in the cultural center not far from downtown. The place had an upstairs and downstairs. It was four to a room but each room had its own bathroom. My roommates and I always kept our room clean. I didn't have any problems out of the girls unlike any of the other places that I was at. I still attended the same high school and worked as much as I could. I started having weekly sessions with the therapist that worked at the group home. I was able to talk to her about my past and the things that I was going through without her passing judgment or making me feel guilty. One of the things I was able to talk to her openly about was being molested. Even though I hated talking or thinking about what happened, she somehow made it easy for me to open up and talk to her.

Eric and I continued dating but I realized he wasn't right for me. I began thinking about the type of person that I was interested in and Eric only fell into two of those categories. He was attractive and able to communicate well; other than that, we didn't have much in common. He stole cars and sold drugs for a living. He had a child when he was 14 by a girl that was 19. He had been through a lot and he was living a rough life. I liked his bad boy mentality. I always felt loved, safe, and secure when I was around him, but I couldn't see myself being with him in the long run. We started dating other people but we kept in touch. In order to have healthy relationships you have to know the characteristics that you are looking for in a companion. Therefore I have listed the 10 most characteristics that people look for in a companion.

Characteristics to look for in a companion.

1. Attraction physically and mentally
2. Ability to communicate
3. Ability to be faithful
4. Compatibility
5. Drive
6. Family orientated
7. Goal orientated
8. Respectful
9. Responsible
10. Spiritually supportive

CHAPTER 17

DEATH & DESTRUCTION

After Eric and I stopped dating, I got a second job that summer and saved close to $2000. My Aunt and Uncle worked with the group home about allowing me to come back and stay with them. I would spend the night at their house on the weekends. A few months later, the court granted them guardianship.

I continued working and going to school. Shortly after Eric and I broke up, I started dating someone else. I met a guy named Maxwell. He had recently graduated from high school and joined the military. He was very attractive and he drove a Lexus. We spent as much time together as we could before he had to go back. He was stationed in Fort Hood, Texas and it was hard being so far away from him but we would talk as much as possible. If I couldn't get in contact with him, I would check with his father to see how he was doing. His father was cool and we got along well. I had not heard from Maxwell in over a week, so I decided to call his father. We talked for awhile and he told me that Maxwell was doing ok. He also asked how the baby was doing and when he would get a chance to see his granddaughter. I kept my composure and went along with everything that he was saying as if I knew what he was talking about. I broke down when we got off the phone. I was hurt and I couldn't believe what I had heard. All types of thoughts went through my head. If Maxwell would have told me that he had a child by another woman, we probably could have gotten pass everything so I had to assume that he didn't tell me for a reason. I was seriously hurt. I was crushed. I had been through similar situations with David, Marlon, Eric, and now him too. I stopped writing and calling Maxwell. I was done. I didn't know what else to do but leave him alone. I figured that if he wanted to be with me he would not have withheld that type of information.

He would call from time to time but I wouldn't answer. I thought about him like crazy but I couldn't get pass what he had done. At this point, I felt like it was me against the world. I continued to focus on school and working. I started going out and enjoying myself. I didn't let anything or anyone get to me. Maxwell continued calling, he even tried to write but I was hurt.

February 24, 1997

What's up Marlena

How are you? Fine, I sincerely do hope. I decided to write you for reason number one I was thinking about you, reason number two because I miss you and reason number three because I haven't heard from you in a while. I want to apologize for all the fucked up shit I've been doing to you and I can understand if you were not to accept my apology and this is straight up because I really do mean it. I don't know when I coming home. I really haven't made any plans to come yet. It'll probably be in May or some shit like that. That's fucked up you didn't call and wish me a happy birthday. It's all good though I will get your ass back in March. Smile. For some reason I know you been up there cheating on me because I can hear it in your voice when I'm on the phone with you. I know you probably think the same shit about me but actually I haven't been, not saying that I'm not because of you but that's just the way I choose to carry the situation. So do you miss me Marlena? Or do I even matter to you anymore? It's like you just kicked a guy to the curb and shit. I don't hear from you, you don't write or nothing. But I still got love for you. I tried to call you but I didn't know where you were at, you know you got about 10 phone numbers. But anyway if you decide to write back, you know where I'm at.

Love you,
Maxwell

After I received Maxwell's letter I didn't know what to think. I wanted to accept his apology but I knew we could never go back to the way things were. He eventually came home for the holiday. We spent time together but I knew I could never trust him like I used to. He and I were supposed to be so much better than that. Eventually, both of us moved on and went in different directions but we kept in touch and saw each other from time to time.

I was out one day and decided to stop by Eric's house. I don't know what it was but for some strange reason, I started thinking about him a lot. I didn't have his number to call anymore so I said I would take my chances and see how he was doing. I knocked on his door but no one answered. As I turned away and got ready to leave, I saw a car pulling up in the driveway. It happened to be his brother. I asked how he was doing and if Eric was around. He looked at me and said Eric was killed about a week ago.

How to deal with death

1. Understand that death is a natural part of life.

2. Understand that death is inevitable.

3. Learn how to manage your emotions.

4. Learn how to cope with life transitions.

5. Enable yourself to deal with tragedy and death.

6. Enable yourself to move forward.

7. Give yourself time.

8. Be the best person that you can be.

9. Talk about your feelings with someone you trust.

10. Seek professional help if necessary.

I was devastated and didn't know how to take the news. Losing a friend or loved one is not easy. People deal with death differently. I spent the next few months focusing on school and work. I didn't talk to anyone or talk about losing Eric. Eventually, I pulled myself together, but it took some time. There is no right or wrong way to deal with death. I listed 10 ways, in which a person can deal with death, but it's always best to seek professional help if needed.

CHAPTER 18

FLAWLESS

1998 was one of the best years of my life. I had a brand new car. I was graduating from high school. I was planning a trip to Daytona Beach, FL and the Bahamas for spring break. I was looking good and feeling great. My biggest worry was who I was taking to the prom. I met a couple more guys at the mall but no one sparked any interest until I met Jason. I wasn't attracted to Jason for his looks. I was more or less attracted to him because he was fun to hang out with. He was a couple years older than me, tall, light-skinned, and an excellent dresser. He had the biggest eyes that I had ever seen and a charming personality. He worked at the mall but that was not our first time seeing each other. The first time we actually met was at a nightclub. Everyone on the eastside would hang out at a music theater called Harpos. They had the best parties and many entertainers performed there. I saw some of the best concerts like LL Cool J, Run DMC; I mean the list goes on.

I was having a birthday party so I decided to invite Jason. The party was held downtown at one of the hottest nightclubs in the city. I had a party promoter, the best food, and one of the greatest DJs around. It was usually college night at the club so I wore black DKNY jeans and a red DKNY baby tee.

The club was packed and I was having the time of my life. Many guys approached me but I kept looking over my shoulder hoping to see Jason. He never showed up. I was a little disappointed but I met a nice guy named A.G. We exchanged numbers and talked until the party ended. A.G. was cool. He said he was a well-known high school athlete but I didn't know who he was. He had a nice smile and a very humble personality for the most part. We continued to talk to each other over the phone but he spent a lot of time at practice. Since prom was approaching, I asked him if he would be my date. He was somewhat reluctant so I didn't press the issue since we went to two different schools.

Jason and I crossed paths at work. I didn't say much because I figured that if he was interested, he would have came to my party but he called me and asked me out. From that point on, we started going out with each other. Things were going ok until we decided to switch cars one night. He was pulled over for driving drunk, he went to jail and my car was impounded. I got my car back that night but he had to stay in jail.

I was pissed at him but I quickly got over it. I forgave him because I had too much going on. I was focused on going to the prom, graduating, and going off to college. We would write each other and I would visit him as often as I could. Jason and I had never clarified our relationship. We were never intimate and we had barely kissed but I found myself thinking about him after each visit.

I didn't do much dating but I would see A.G. every once in a while. He was in every major newspaper and was getting ready to go off to school on a basketball scholarship. I liked him and he was nice to me but it was hard for us to pursue anything with each other because his schedule was very demanding. I didn't understand that at the time and started developing feelings for Jason.

Friday, May 15, 1998

Dear Marlena

How are you doing baby girl? I was so happy you came to see me today. I couldn't wait to sit down with a pen and paper. I was so surprised you brought J with you. I kind of needed that. You know what I mean? I guess it's just a guy thing. On the other hand you seem to be confused about us. When I get out nothing is going to change. I promise. I love and care about you so much that I couldn't see myself hurting you in any type of way. I regret so much that I have done especially not being able to be with you on your prom night. I know we are going to do something special the day that I get out just me and you. I feel like we were meant for each other. I can tell because the feelings I have for you are strong enough to last a lifetime. If things don't turn out the way we would like them to, I would never want to lose you as my friend because we were friends before we were anything else. Right? To add to that note our friendship and relationship is going to work out no matter what. I'm asking you not to get discouraged because I know myself better than anyone and I know that I want it to work between us. As for my mother, I'm not going to keep you in the dark about how she makes me feel. I have two brothers, the oldest one been in jail since I was nine. My other brother Sean was the middle son and the only brother I really ever had. My father was a dead beat dad so I didn't have a relationship with him. When me and Sean got older, Sean's father started coming back around. He began talking about marrying my mom and telling lies all the time. To make a long story short, my mother began acting like she loved my brother more than she loved me. When my brother got killed last July I really knew it was true. She loved that fool more than she loved me. That's alright though. That's why I keep my distance. I know I only got one mother, but she stop caring for me when I was in the 11th grade. She lost faith in me. She kept saying I wasn't going to finish high school like my brothers. Since then I have done everything to prove her wrong. She stopped caring that is what hurt me the most. I'll never do that to my kids for nobody. You wanted to know so I'm telling you. As much as I did for her, when I could have been thinking about myself. She just did something to my heart that can't be healed. Enough, I'm lost for words right now so until the next letter I love you baby girl.

Love Always,

Jason

P.S. Sorry I ended the letter this way. Write me back soon.

Monday, June 29, 1998

Dear Marlena

How you doing? I hope everything is going all right for you, being that you got so much on your mind. I've been alright, despite you telling me that you might not be able to wait for me. I didn't get upset about it because I kind of expected it but much sooner. I hate that we really didn't get a chance to do much together. I was reading all of the letters you wrote and I came across a sentence, "Before you got locked up I thought you were perfect." What did you mean by that? I'm not perfect anymore because I got locked up? I'm not tripping cause I could have told you that I wasn't perfect. The closer my court date gets the more depressed I get. I believe it's because I know the more time I get, the more we are going to grow apart. It ain't your fault, so I don't blame you for going your way. I just should have had my shit together before I got involved with you. Then again my letters haven't been the most exciting or cheerful. I'm going to always love you and wish the best for you. I will never go a day without remembering you were the one that helped me when I needed it the most. I'm saying all of this because I talked to my mother today and when I asked about you she said you came by and you looked worried. I never seen you look that way before and I hope it wasn't because of me. Don't let me be the reason you are worried, please. I hope I return home soon because I don't want to lose you.

Love,
Jason

P.S. I'm keeping you in my heart and on my mind.

Jason and I learned a lot about each other as time passed. I continued focusing on school and preparing for college. I applied for a few colleges and scholarships, but I knew where I was going to school. I wanted to attend the University of Michigan. I remember visiting the campus in Ann Arbor when I was younger. Marlon had also told me so much about the school that I wanted to experience it for myself. Marlon and I had lost contact but I had a feeling that it wouldn't be for long. One of my close friends CiCi was accepted so I was definitely going. I would focus on school during the day, work at night and party on the weekend.

How to prepare for college

1. Discuss your plans with your parent/guardian or the person closest to you.
2. Work closely with your instructors and counselor to make college an attainable goal if necessary.
3. Prepare and schedule a time to take the SAT exam and other exams if necessary.
4. Visit as many college campuses as possible.
5. Request application materials from all the schools that may be of interest.
6. Apply for financial aid as soon as possible if needed.
7. Apply for as many scholarships as possible.
8. Create a portfolio, which contains the following information for easy access: recommendation letters, transcripts, SAT exam scores, Student Aid Report, an essay and a copy of your diploma/GED.
9. Stay involved in extracurricular activities.
10. Maintain a high grade point average but remember to have fun.

I established a closer relationship with my family before I left for college. We tried to keep in touch as much as possible. I was especially proud of all of my siblings. We all had our different obstacles but we were managing to make it through. My aunt and uncle left Detroit and moved to Tennessee. I was officially on my own. I started college 2 weeks after I graduated from high school.

Preparing for college can be challenging so I listed 10 ways in which a person can prepare for college. All of the suggestions that I have listed may not apply to you. Whether you are going to college for the first time or returning to school getting a good education is very important. The best advice that anyone has ever given me was to get a good education. Learning is priceless. People have given their lives for the opportunity to read and learn so I hope that at least one person is influenced to further their education.

CHAPTER 19

EARS THAT HEAR &
EYES THAT SEE

I missed my aunt, uncle, and cousins but I was also enjoying my freedom. Jason was released from jail a few weeks after I started college. I came home for the weekend and I was there the first day he got out. It was awkward being able to spend time with him. I was accustomed to the glass window being between us and talking over a phone. The awkwardness quickly went away and we had sex for the first time. It was nothing like I imagined it would be and I'm sure he felt the same way because he asked me if I was a virgin.

My first semester of college was a breeze. My second semester was not that easy. I found out that I was pregnant and I was scared out of my mind. I didn't know what I was going to do. I had just become fully responsible for myself so I knew I wasn't ready to take care of another human being. I thought about getting an abortion because I thought that having an abortion would make things easier on me financially. I always wanted children so I knew I would never be able to live with the guilt of killing my first child. I even thought about giving my child up for adoption but when I thought of the things I experienced in foster care, I chose to take care of my child by myself. Jason and I weren't on the best terms. I found out he was cheating with other women. I was insecure and we were always arguing. We even got into a fight during Labor Day weekend about his drinking. We were fighting on the side of the road and luckily, some men pulled over and pulled him off me. I thought they were going to beat him half to death. I didn't want to leave him but I wasn't about to be a fool either. I went to the hospital and the police came but I didn't press charges.

My pregnancy was horrible. I was sick every day. A.G. came to see me one time and I threw up right in front of him. He was so sweet and I felt so bad. Deep down in my heart I felt like him and I should have been together. He told me that he was transferring schools and only going to be 10 minutes away from me. I wanted to cry after he left because I realized he was a great guy. I kept telling myself repeatedly that maybe it wasn't meant to be anyway because if it was we would be together. We talked on the phone frequently but we lost contact after the semester was over. I transferred campuses and moved back to the city so that I could prepare myself to be a mother.

How to prepare for parenthood

1. Seek adequate prenatal care as early as possible.

2. Eat a well balanced diet and take prenatal vitamins.

3. Get as much rest as possible.

4. Create a schedule or daily routine and follow it as closely as possible.

5. Make a list of all of the things the baby and expectant mother will need during the first year.

6. Prepare a realistic budget for all the things that are needed during the first year, then come up with a time frame and ideas to gather those items.

7. Take parenting courses if possible.

8. Create a parenting plan if necessary.

9. Keep a scrap or memory book of the entire experience to share with friends, family, and the child once he or she is of age.

10. Make the most out of the parenting experience because children grow up fast.

Being pregnant and trying to make a home for my unborn child and myself was tedious. I had a hard time getting on my feet. My car got repossessed. I even found myself homeless at one point but my co-workers and friends started helping me out. I bought another car and I started working back at my old job in the mall. I didn't want any handouts but I got as much help as I could get. I told as few people as possible. I knew everyone that had believed in me over the years would probably be disappointed but I was a young adult so it really didn't matter. My child was a gift no matter how people felt. Even though I wanted to have children, I prayed and vowed never to get pregnant again until I was married. I had no clue about what it took to be a good mother. I also knew that being a parent wasn't going to be easy. I listed 10 things that helped me as a new parent and I hope this information can help someone else.

CHAPTER 20

LEAN NOT ON YOUR OWN UNDERSTANDING

Eventually, things started working out for me. One of the scholarship foundations found out that I was pregnant and started assisting me so that I can finish school. A few months after my daughter was born, I moved into a two-bedroom apartment. The apartment was decent and was fairly close to campus. Being a new parent was hard but I had plenty of help. My mentor from the scholarship foundation assisted me with childcare. Her mother would keep my daughter while I went to school and worked.

I started dating again. I met a guy named Randy. He was younger than me but I liked him a lot. The first timed he called, I didn't know where things would go so I told him I lived at home with my mom and I definitely didn't tell him I had a daughter. By the end of the conversation, he told me he was 17 and I told him the truth about me. I let him know that I didn't stay with my mom, I was 19 and I had a daughter. We dated off and on for a couple years but he stayed in and out of trouble for selling drugs.

January 28, 2000

Marlena,

I apologize for not writing you. I've been busy a lot. Baby I want you to know that I love you and I need you in my life. You've been by my side from the start. I think about the things you have said to me and it lets me know you really care about me. I know it's meant for us to be together and that's what we are going to do but you have to know this. I only want to be with you and I will always love you from the bottom of my heart. There are a lot of things that I want in life and I need someone by my side. Someone to hold on to and that person is you. I know that I am not there to keep you by my side now but I want you to be faithful to me because I'm giving you my heart so please leave it in one piece.

Love always,
Randy

Randy and I would write it each other as much as possible. I even went to see him a few times. Things were going rather well until I ran into Maxwell one day. It was good seeing him but I knew I would have hell on my hands if Randy found out about me talking to Maxwell; so I made it perfectly clear to him that I was involved with someone. He didn't seem to have a problem with that and we never crossed the line with each other. I would let him come over to my place and hang out. We started hanging out with each other more and more. I could tell that there was some attraction there but I wasn't going to try to pursue anything with him again until I knew what was up between Randy and me.

Easter was coming around and Randy was scheduled to come home. Randy and I planned to go to church together. I didn't hear from him the day before Easter so I wasn't sure what was going on. Maxwell had also stayed over my house the day before. I was somewhat worried because I didn't want Randy to come over while Maxwell was around so I told Maxwell that he had to leave. He said he understood and I was relieved. No sooner than Maxwell left, I started getting ready for church and Randy came through the door. I was so happy to see him. Next thing I knew, Maxwell was at the door again. He said he left something. Randy got pissed and took off. I tried to explain, but Randy wasn't trying to hear it. I felt so foolish, but I knew I hadn't did anything wrong. I soaked it up as a lesson learned. I didn't understand why Maxwell would do such a thing but it wasn't the first time that he played me so I wasn't too surprised. Maxwell called and apologized later that night and of course, I forgave him like an idiot.

The next morning, I started my day as I usually do. I went to work later on that afternoon and by the time I got home, I was tired and ready to go to sleep. As soon as I got out my car, I saw Maxwell pulling up. I was shocked to see him but I didn't trip out and start acting all crazy like I wanted to. He asked if he could come in. I said that

I was tired. He said he was leaving in the morning going down south with his father and he would appreciate it if he could come in and talk. I said all right. We talked for a while and I didn't want to be rude so I told him he could stay and sleep in the living room. I took my daughter in my room, closed the door and laid down. When I woke up, Maxwell had stolen everything from out my place. He stole my computer, printer, copier, scanner, a $1500 necklace, and everything else that he could carry out. I didn't know what to do. I called the police and Randy's sister. She told me I could bring my daughter over and go to the police station to make a police report.

Luckily, I had renter's insurance. The insurance company sent me a check to replace everything in a matter of days. I used the insurance money to move and replace my things. I moved into a house that Randy's cousin owned. Even though Randy and I weren't on the best terms, I figured that would be a good move because his cousin was willing to sell the house to me at a reasonable price once I got enough money to purchase it.

A lot happened over the next year. I started to mature mentally and embrace my womanhood but my life was difficult and it often got very hectic. I was a single mother, full-time student, and full-time employee. I was also determined and not going to let anything stand in my way of finishing school. There were times when I got depressed and just wanted to give up and didn't see the point in finishing school.

I started focusing on other things in life like the police academy and the military. I proudly passed the agility and written exam for the police academy. I almost went to the military, but for some reason, things didn't feel right. I didn't feel like that was my destiny. After awhile, I realized that the most important thing for me to do was to be there for my daughter and continue my education.

My grades dropped very low and I often felt like I was a failure but then I would reflect back over everyone that paved the way for me to get an education. I knew that getting a good education was important, but I soon began to realize that my most important reason for going to school was to learn. I was always told to go to school and get a good education so that I could get a good job, but no one actually stressed the importance of going to school to learn. I began to focus on me while embracing my education. I didn't agree with everything that I was being taught, but I accepted it because it made me a well rounded individual. There were many times when I felt like giving up, but I refused to let anything get the best of me. I kept my spirits high and continued to push forward. I listed 10 general ways in which a person can lift their spirits, but you can create your own list and refer back to it as needed.

How to lift your spirit

1. Do GOD's work every day!
2. Meditate, pray and worship every day!
3. Take a walk, exercise or get involved in extracurricular activities!
4. Visit or spend time with family and friends!
5. Get a new hairstyle or haircut!
6. Have a manicure & pedicure!
7. Go out to eat!
8. Go to a movie, play, or special event!
9. Go shopping for a couple of new things!
10. Take a vacation.

CHAPTER 21

NO HARM BEFALLS THE RIGHTEOUS

Jason would call from time to time. Things weren't the best but I wasn't going to complain. I started to feel a void and a little lost. This wasn't the first time that I had felt like this. Most of it had to do with the fact that I was overwhelmed with being a mom and my on again off again friendship with her father didn't make things any better. In fact, I think it made matters worse. I couldn't see myself being in a relationship or being intimate with him again after all that we had been through but I did try to keep the lines of communication open for our daughter.

I started seeing someone else. I met a guy named Lawrence. He was five or six years older than me. We went out several times. He met some of my family. I met his mother and his brother. He treated me like a queen and he was very protective of me but he was married. I couldn't be involved with a married man so I cut him off. It hurt like hell but I had to do it.   Jason called one day and I was just about done with him wanting to be a father whenever he pleased. The last straw was in October of 2001. He asked if I could bring our daughter to see him. I explained to him that I was going to attend a funeral but I would be glad to bring her by afterwards. He called all day like he was crazy until I told him I was on my way. When I finally arrived at his house, I knocked on the door but no one answered. I started knocking again until I heard the door unlock. Jason stood in the door with nothing on but boxer shorts. I asked him if he was busy and he said "I'm getting ready to go." I started questioning him about what was going on and why he asked us to come over if he knew he was about to leave. He said that he was getting dressed and we would have to come back another time. We began arguing back and forth. I was pissed. He then slammed the door in my face.   I was furious; I began beating on the door and window so hard that the glass cracked.

When I came to my senses and realized what I had done, I turned around to walk back to the car. A few seconds later, I was being hit over the head with a pistol. He was yelling at me and I screamed at my sister, who was in the car, for help. I asked him if he was actually going to kill me in front of his daughter, but he didn't respond. Instead, he kept hitting me until my sister talked him out of beating me to death. We immediately drove to the police station to file a complaint. The next day, I went to court to have a restraining order filed against him.

We went to court a few times, he plead guilty, and was sentenced to 1-year probation, anger management, and no violent contact with me.

After everything was said and done, I thought about Lawrence, but I couldn't get in touch with him. It had been months since we'd talked. I just couldn't stop thinking about him so I decided to take a chance and go by his mother's house. I remembered the house from when he took me to meet her. She answered the door, we talked for a while and she told me that he was in jail. He was pulled over by the police and he had a gun in his car. She gave me the address to where he was, I decided to write him, and he wrote me back.

10/17/01

Hi,

I'm glad to know that you and Jada are doing well. You cross my mind all the time, but I didn't want to be a bother. Thanks for the picture. Both of you look very nice and happy. I always wanted to see you with a smile. I'm doing just fine. I'll be home next summer. I know you are wondering why I'm locked up. I finally got caught carrying a gun. I'm through with the street shit, just work and home from here on out. I'm shocked to hear from you, I thought that you had really turned your back on me after our last encounter. I didn't have any hard feelings towards you I just thought you found someone that you wanted to be with. I don't know why you wouldn't expect me to write or call you, I had no hard feelings about what your choice was, I just always wondered why? Could you answer that for me? On a different subject you are about to be finished with school soon. That should take a load off of you. Your new job sounds pretty interesting too. So who is the lucky guy in our life? Have you spoken to your Aunt? I know that you have a life to live and business to attend to but I hope to hear from you more often if possible. Knowing that I am thought about from someone on the outside of this fence means more than words can explain. I hope from here on out we will keep in touch, try to regain what we had and hopefully move forward. If you have a man in your life let me know because I don't want to cause conflict in your life.

Lawrence

P. S.

Thanks for your prayers!

Lawrence and I continued writing each other and I started going to visit him up state. We talked about our plans for the future. He had a good job before he got locked up, but he wasn't certain if he would be able to go back to work after he was out. He said he wanted to start his own business so I started sending books about starting a business to him. Things were going well. He and his wife got divorced. We started making plans to be together, but I couldn't deal with the distance between us. He didn't have an exact date on when he was going to be released. I started listening to other people tell me that he wasn't good for me, etc., so I stopped writing him and kept focusing on school, going to work, and being a mother.

I had huge dreams of owning my own business one day. By assisting Lawrence, I learned a lot about being an entrepreneur. I listed 10 steps a person should take when starting a business because entrepreneurship is important and the rewards of starting a business are great.

How to start a business

1. Assess your strengths and weaknesses.
2. Create a business name.
3. Decide on a business location.
4. Create a business plan.
5. File paperwork designating the type of legal entity.
6. Obtain an employer identification number.
7. Obtain business license and permits if necessary.
8. Establish a team of professionals such as an accountant, banker, lawyer, etc.
9. Obtain business supplies and marketing materials.
10. Set an official grand opening date.

CHAPTER 22

EVEN IN LAUGHTER THE HEART MAY ACHE

I worked, went to school, took care of my daughter to the best of my ability, and focused on starting a business as a consultant in my spare time. I also started dating again, even though I seemed to attract all the wrong men. Things were no different when I met Charles. He was not what I expected in a man nor was he what I wanted but we started off as friends. For the most part, he was always there for me. When things got hard and every time I needed him, he was right there. When my car broke down, he got it fixed. When my phone got cut off, he gave me a cell phone. When my daughter and I didn't have food to eat, he made sure we were fed. He was fun to be around, but I wasn't attracted to him. Many times when we would go out in public, I found myself embarrassed because I wanted someone with more class and sophistication, but I began to accept him for who he was. I learned to appreciate him. We lived in the same area and associated with some of the same people. In fact, one of our mutual associates was murdered. We went through a lot together and at one point, we even stopped speaking to each other for a short period after I called his phone and another woman answered. She had the nerve to question me as if I called her phone so we exchanged words. I found the whole thing amusing at first. I didn't understand how he could show so much interest in me but allow another woman to answer his phone. I couldn't believe she had the nerve to disrespect me like that. I was even more shocked that he did not intervene, but I guess he was trying to prove a point. After some time had passed and I started looking back over the situation and realizing how much he meant to me, I didn't find the situation as amusing so I decided to drop by to see him. We had an opportunity to talk and everything went well.

From that point on, I decided that I was going to take him seriously and give him an opportunity to grow on me. I ended up giving into him and our first sexual experience together was pleasurable. From that moment on, I thought I was in love with him and he was my best friend. We started getting our priorities in order and ended up moving in together. I encouraged him to stay out of the streets and go back to school to get his GED. He managed to listen and he was enrolled in college 3 months after that. He did well his first semester and picked up a couple of jobs along the way. One job was a seasonal position working for the post office and the other was a work-study job. Things were going good for a while, but I knew in my heart that I wanted to be with someone else.

A few of my friends and family members didn't approve of him because they felt that I deserved someone better but I didn't care because I knew that I really cared about him even though there were things that I didn't even like about him. I have never been the type of person that is particularly drawn to people for what they have. I have to be drawn to the person mentally. I have to have an interest in the person beyond their physical appearance. I didn't want to change him; I just wanted him to know that there was more to life. He didn't have any goals or dreams. He acted like there was no hope for his future, but he treated me well. At one point, he showered me with cards and flowers. He would give me the world if he had it and always made me feel like no other women existed. I couldn't do anything but accept him for who he was because his upbringing was similar to mine. He had been through a lot as a kid and I could identify with everything that he went through. In fact, we were even in the same group home at one point. Although there were some signs that things might not work between us because he was going in one direction and I was going in another, it was hard for us to end the relationship. He was set in his ways and I was set in mine but I wasn't going to turn my back on him. We had our ups and downs, but I accepted our differences for what they were and decided to keep moving forward.

Despite his lack of goals and ambitions, he was very supportive of my plans even when things did not go as planned. I was able to successfully obtain my education without worrying too much about all the household responsibilities. I had several challenges as an entrepreneur and wanted to quit on many occasions. Since I did not come from a wealthy family and I was not the heiress of a family owned business, I had to make a lot of financial sacrifices.

How to close a business

1. Establish an agreement and written authorization to dissolve the business entity.
2. Create an exit strategy, timeline and task list of things to do before closing the business.
3. Create a team or group of professionals that are able to assist with completing tasks.
4. Inform all interested parties such as customers, vendors and suppliers, professional service providers, consultants, trade groups, employees, media, creditors, and contractors that the business is closing. This should be done through the release of announcements and notices.
5. Formally close out all business operations and sales on a specific date.
6. Review the listing of assets and conduct a physical inventory.
7. File Articles of Dissolution, which formally terminates the business with most state licensing departments.
8. Obtain tax clearance notice.
9. Close bank accounts for business.
10. Maintain and store business records.

Working full time, going to school full time, taking care of a child, managing a household, and running a business was a lot to take on at one time. There were days when I didn't know if I was coming or going but I had to make a better life for my family. I would get discouraged often. I not only failed in many of my relationships, but I also failed at business a few times so I have listed 10 steps a person should take when closing a business because closing out a business properly is just as important as starting a new business.

CHAPTER 23

HOPE DEFERRED MAKES THE HEART SICK

Things were going all right between Charles and me for the most part. He was a big help around the house. I didn't have to work as much and I was able to concentrate on school more. We did many things together as a family. My daughter had recently turned three years old and we enrolled her in preschool. We also put her in various activities. She started taking dance lessons and later on, she began taking golf, karate, and music lessons. I would volunteer at her preschool on a regular basis. I even participated on the parent board.

Volunteering was a big responsibility and very demanding at times, but I enjoyed it and formed many friendships with the other parents. We would go out of town to training conferences from time to time. On one particular occasion, I went out of town and when I came back, I received a letter from Lawrence. I was completely caught off guard and a few old feelings resurfaced.

9/30/03

Marlena,

How are you doing? I'm doing just fine! I know that I haven't written you or tried to contact you in awhile. My time was too long to try and keep hold of you from in here so I did what was best for the both of us and let you go your way without trying to interfere. But as you can see if you have been on the computer lately, I'll be home in 5 more months. I'm still waiting on some paperwork. If you aren't busy, I would like to hear from you. Let me know what has changed and what's going on with you. I'll write you back soon because I have a lot to tell you.

Take care,
Lawrence

I never responded to Lawrence's letter because I tried to make things work with Charles. We started a life together and things were going well. I didn't want to risk damaging my relationship, so I continued focusing on everything else I had going on. I would think about Lawrence from time to time but that was it. He stopped by one day when he first came home but I wasn't there. Charles answered the door. Charles didn't get upset. We had a small talk when I got back home, but that was all. Keeping my family together became my biggest priority. Nothing else mattered at that point. In addition to focusing on the obligations and responsibilities that I already had, I started dedicating even more of my time to volunteering. Volunteering was rewarding and gratified me. I valued my involvement with my daughter's

~ 142 ~

preschool program and I took my volunteer opportunity seriously.

My daughter's preschool program opened some wonderful doors for me. It even gave me an opportunity to travel and learn some very valuable parenting skills. I listed 10 ways in which a person can be an effective volunteer and I hope that people will donate a portion of their time to help worthy causes like Head Start and other charitable organizations.

How to be an effective volunteer

1. Research the organization before you commit to being a volunteer.
2. Volunteer for an organization that interests you.
3. Volunteer for an organization that you believe in and feel passionate about.
4. Take your volunteer position seriously.
5. Establish a good relationship with the organization you are volunteering for.
6. Make sure you have adequate time to volunteer.
7. Be sure to attend suggested/recommended trainings and meetings.
8. Make the most of your volunteer experience.
9. Encourage other people to get involved and volunteer.
10. Resign from your volunteer position when you are no longer able to meet the volunteer requirements or loose passion for the cause.

CHAPTER 24

HE SAID, SHE SAID

Some days were crazy and more out of control than others were. In December of 2003, I was finally going to graduate from college. So much was happening for me. I was serving as the chairperson for the parent board, as well as traveling and attending different events. Things seemed to be going well until Jason called one day. I was caught off guard at first, but when we started talking to each other, it seemed as if we were still the best of friends. He made plans to come visit Jada, but never showed up. The next thing I knew, he was viciously murdered.

It had only been a month since Jada's father was killed. I was still shaken up and confused about how it all happened. One minute I was focused on getting ready to graduate, then not even one minute later, my attention was on the murder of my daughter's father. I didn't know what happened, but I was definitely eager to find out. The more I found out, the more pain I felt. It turns out that Jason was probably robbed and beaten to death.

Earlier that day, Jason had gotten away with taking over $150,000 from a department store. The money was supposed to be picked up by armed security and deposited into the bank, but Jason and his accomplice intercepted it instead. No one was ever the wiser until it was too late. I was really torn up about the whole situation.

Charles stood by me through the whole thing. He was always a great father to Jada so we decided to get married that year in July. It took about four months to plan everything out and it turned out ok despite the short planning and lack of money. I didn't ask for a lot of help from my family and friends because I knew that a lot of them didn't approve of our relationship. I invited everyone I could think of and get in touch with.

I started to get worried and frustrated the closer it got towards our wedding day because I really wanted things to be special, but it seemed like everything was working against us. I started going to the casino and gambling away money that I didn't have. I started feeling empty and depressed. Charles and I continued to press forward and to my surprise, things began to work themselves out.

How to prepare for marriage

1. Know your companion's needs.
2. Close out all past relationships with a good understanding.
3. Discuss family planning.
4. Have an agreement regarding the wedding ceremony and the date.
5. Establish a budget for the wedding.
6. Conduct a debt analysis.
7. Establish a budget for your new household.
8. Have a prenuptial agreement.
9. Seek premarital counseling.
10. Inform family and friends.

Wedding Check List

✓		Cost
	1. Engagement & Wedding Rings	
	2. Wedding Gown, Shoes, Jewelry, & Accessories	
	3. Tuxedo, Shoes, & Accessories	
	4. Engagement Parties	
	5. Ceremony & Reception Hall	
	6. Announcements, Invitations, & Thank You Cards	
	7. Bridesmaids' Dresses	
	8. Groomsmen Tuxedo	
	9. Marriage License	
	10. DJ/ Band	
	11. Photographer	
	12. Videographer	
	13. Florist	
	14. Food/Caterer/Wedding Cake/ Misc	
	15. Honeymoon	
	16. Hair/Nails/Pedicure/Facial/Makeover	
	17. Rehearsal Dinner	
	18. Bachelor Party	
	19. Bridal Shower/Bachelorette Party	
	20. Decorations & Misc.	
	Total	

Marriage is a huge commitment. It is a lifetime partnership and it should be treated as such. Preparing for that special day is a very big task so I created a checklist and listed 10 ways in which a person can prepare for marriage. A formal wedding ceremony may not be important to everyone, however, there are a few essential elements that every bride and groom must have.

Charles and I had some very trying times right after we got married. He started back hanging in the streets. He caught a couple of drug charges. He was in and out of jail. I even had a letter come to the house from the State in regards to an aggravated sexual offense charge that he was supposed to register for. He caught the case when he was around 13 or 14 and he never told me. I told him about my past and that I was molested. He knew the person that molested me and he even knew that I forgave that person. I was pissed and it was hard for me to get past everything so we separated for a few days. We eventually got back together and I stood by him because we both wanted to work things out. Shortly after we got back together, I found out I was pregnant.

CHAPTER 25

EACH HEART KNOWS ITS OWN BITTERNESS

We made it through another year. There were a few bumps and bruises along the way but we made it. I started Graduate school and we had a child on the way. Things seemed to be getting better until my intuition started telling me that Charles was cheating on me. At first, I didn't believe it or better yet, I didn't want to believe it. We hadn't even been married a year yet, so I refused to believe it. I pushed those thoughts to the back of my mind and forced myself to believe that he could not be cheating on me that soon. I knew that men cheated on their wives and women often cheated on their husbands, but all I could say was "damn." Could he really be cheating on me while I'm pregnant with his first child?

I reflected over every relationship I had ever been in. I reflected over my mother's failed marriage and all of her past relationships. I reflected over my father's failed marriage. I reflected over every relationship and every marriage that I had ever known about. I wanted to know what made them work and what made them fail.

My suspicions were eventually confirmed shortly after I gave birth to our daughter, Joy. We were on our way to Joy's one-month doctor's appointment when the girl started calling my phone. I blew up and was ready to go off. We argued and fought about the situation but there was nothing that either one of us could do to take back what happened. He tried to break it off with her and didn't know how, so she started calling my phone and threatening him.

I had a choice to make and it was one of the hardest decisions that I have ever had to make. The decision seemed easy at first. I thought about just getting a divorce, raising my children by myself, and moving on with my life, but the more that I tried to move on, the more difficult it became. My whole life revolved around being a family. Everything I ever accomplished was for kids and my husband. I could eventually get over the cheating and the betrayal, but I couldn't decide if he was worth it. I couldn't decide if he deserved another chance. My friends and family told me to just let the marriage end, but I still cared about him. I had a newborn to think about, so I decided to try and make it work, again.

I knew the odds were against me but I refused to give up. I was determined to make our marriage work because I was tired of feeling like a failure. I almost failed college, my relationship with my parents failed, my past relationships failed so the last thing I wanted was a failed marriage. I was a fighter. I always put up a fight when it came to getting what I wanted so keeping my marriage together would be no different.

We eventually decided to stay together and move forward. I started balancing my time between my family and my career. We started making even more plans for our future. We started setting more goals and reevaluating our finances. We tried to manage and budget our money as best as possible.

Although we lived together and discussed our finances before we got married, we never thoroughly talked about budgeting and managing our finances the way we should have. We had a few tough times but we worked together as a team. Money wasn't a big issue in our marriage but there were definitely some financial aspects within the marriage that I wish I could go back and do differently. Many marriages fall apart or fail because of money, so I have listed a basic budget of monthly expenses, as well as 10 ways in which a person can effectively manage their finances. This information will vary of course depending on the individual and amount of each expense, but the purpose is to gain a general understanding of how to manage major expenses.

Monthly Budget

Expense	Amount
House Payment/Rent	
Water	
Gas	
Electricity	
Cable/Internet	
Phone Bill	
Groceries/ Food	
Cell Phone	
Car Note	
Insurance	
Fuel/Gas	
Student Loans/Personal Loans	
Credit Card Bills	
Misc. Expenses	
Emergency cash	
Total	

How to manage your finances

1. Create a budget.

2. Track your expenses.

3. Save, Save, Save.

4. Manage your resources wisely.

5. Live within your means.

6. Pay cash.

7. Create multiple streams of income.

8. Invest in your family.

9. Invest in yourself.

10. Get insurance.

CHAPTER 26

THE ADULTERER

Things continued going okay between Charles and I. We would occasionally have disagreements about other women. I sensed that he was still cheating but I let it go until I had proof. I had a lot to look forward to. I decided I was going to make some changes in my life so I began to take a good look at myself. I started thinking about my life and how far I had come compared to where I came from. I thought about what I wanted to do in life and the things I wanted to accomplish. I had already made a few accomplishments such as a Bachelor's Degree in Public Relations and Master's Degree in Business Administration.

I continued volunteering for my daughter's preschool program until she transitioned into kindergarten. Then I accepted a position as a family service worker for the Head Start program. I encountered more women and children that came from similar backgrounds and experiences as me.

Those experiences allowed me to grow into a better person and inspired me to do more for others.

Although I loved the relationships that I built in the Head Start program, after a few years, I decided it was time for me to move on. I wanted to go back to school and pursue a career in nursing. Charles and I talked things over and we agreed that we should eventually move south; so I started applying to colleges in Atlanta. I continued working at Head Start for about two years, but the excitement was gone and I didn't feel like I was making a difference anymore. It became very stressful at times. Funding for the program was always being cut and it seemed as if we could never do enough to help the children and families we served.

I didn't want to leave my friends and family behind but I was stressed out and needed a fresh start. I ran into a few people from my past like Marlon, who happened to be teaching at a college. I also found out A.G. started playing professional football for the NFL. There were a few signs that told me not to go but I overlooked them. I even had a mental breakdown a few weeks before it was time for us to move from all of the stress. I found out Charles was cheating on me again. I could not believe that after all the sacrifices that I had made for our family that he would have the nerve to cheat on me again. I wanted to choke the life out of him. My family and friends helped me get through it. I forgave him and let the whole situation go.

How to manage stress

1. Meditate.

2. Exercise.

3. Get a massage.

4. Listen to soft or calming music.

5. Slow down.

6. Pace yourself.

7. Don't neglect your health.

8. Don't over-extend yourself.

9. Get adequate rest.

10. Seek professional help if necessary.

In addition to the problems that I experienced at work, the problems in my marriage also resurfaced. I became overwhelmingly stressed out and did not know how to deal with it. Eventually, I learned that some stress is a natural part of life. There is good stress and bad stress so we have to deal with it accordingly. It just all depends on how you handle it. I listed 10 ways in which a person can manage their stress. You can create your own list and refer to it as needed.

As for me, I used to deal with stress by continuing to move forward when obstacles stood in my way. I inherited this characteristic from my mother. I would hold things in until it was just too much for me to take. At that point, I would go off like a ticking time bomb or go into a deep depression just like my mother. The idea of seeking professional help never bothered me; I actually liked it because I needed someone to talk to. Most of the therapist pacified me and told me that many of the things that I was going through was normal, especially considering all that I had been through. There were a few that suggested medicine for depression, but I was against it. I did not want medicine regulating my energy or me because I saw what it did to my mother. I also knew that taking medicine improperly could lead to a premature death. Look at what happened to Anna Nicole Smith and Michael Jackson. Drugs are something that I could definitely do without. I would rather have a glass of wine and a hot bath to ease my mind.

CHAPTER 27

DO WHAT IS RIGHT & JUST

After finally moving to Atlanta, finding a job, and being adjusted to our new place, most of my stress went away. We had a few challenges and a few issues getting our finances situated. I had to put my dreams of going back to school to be a nurse on hold because I couldn't pay for all my classes, so I took a class to be certified as a nursing assistant instead. After successfully completing my certification as a nursing assistant, I got a job working at a hospice doing home visits. Aside from all the driving, it was a decent job and I had a good relationship with all of my patients. I planned to work as a nursing assistant until I was able to save my money and return to school to become a registered nurse, but something always came up.

One evening, Charles decided to stay out all night. I was fed up and I couldn't take it anymore. When he finally arrived, we had a lengthy disagreement and I asked him to leave. He refused and stated he had nowhere else to go. I became angry and told him he could go back to the same place he stayed at all night. I picked up the phone to call the police because he was not being cooperative. I did not want to take the law into my own hands and I certainly did not want to leave because I was the one going to work everyday and keeping a roof over our heads. He failed to realize that I stayed up all night worrying about him. He knew I had to go to work the next morning and if something would have happened that would have been one more thing for me to worry about. I was under a lot of pressure at work and at home. I felt as if I was being under paid at work and unappreciated at home.

After several minutes of arguing, our neighbor finally instructed Charles to go ahead and leave until I had time to calm down. It was a good thing that he left because the police showed up shortly after that. I told them that everything was resolved and it was just a misunderstanding but they insisted on coming in. I explained what happened and told them that I had no other choice but to request for him to leave because if I allowed him to stay, the situation probably would have escalated into something serious. I knew that I had a very bad temper and a low tolerance for foolishness. The police decided to blow the whole thing out of proportion and bring charges against him. That was something that I definitely did not want. We had both experienced and overcome years of childhood abuse and trauma. The last thing I wanted was for our marriage to fail, but it was becoming more and more apparent that we both were taking different roads in life.

Despite everything that I had accomplished and was trying to accomplish, I had a difficult time dealing with foolishness and I felt that some of Charles's actions were very foolish; however, I stood by him until the case was over because I knew that staying out all night did not warrant the untruths that were being told against him by the police. I could not honestly allow him to plead guilty or be found guilty of something he simply did not do. The police had an opportunity to speak with him on the day that the incident took place, but they made up a different story for whatever reason. I actually called next door to our neighbor's house in the presence of the police and had a lengthy discussion with Charles, but they were not interested in hearing what actually happened.

I cooperated with the law as much as possible and I explained to the police, as well as the prosecutor that the charges were false and that he did not do anything wrong. I also explained to them that Charles has been through enough and made several mistakes in life, but he did not deserve to be prosecuted for something he did not do. It was bad enough that he was later arrested and had to spend a week in jail over this whole situation. I understood that domestic violence is a serious matter and these matters are not taken lightly, I also knew that sometimes these matters are over exaggerated to prove a case or a point and this was something that I did not want to be a part of.

When I called the police, my intentions were to have Charles removed before I did something that I would later regret. When the police arrived, I tried my best to explain to them that the situation was under control but they continued to pursue the matter.

It was a very unfortunate situation because what Charles and I experienced was a simple disagreement, which is common for many families. I tried to do the best that I could for my family. I felt like I had done everything that society expected me to do and I still could not get ahead. I was drained emotionally and all that I expected was for my husband to be supportive and stay on the right track for our children. I wrote a letter to the judge explaining how I felt about the situation and the case was later dropped.

Tuesday, May 22, 2007

Attention: Judge Alex J. Wong

RE: Case # 07C85639

To Whom It May Concern,

This letter is to inform you of the pending case #07C85639 against Charles Leon Mayes is frivolous and over exaggerated. Mr. Mayes is not a threat to our children or me and he has never threatened to harm us. The police report does not accurately reflect the incident and chain of events that took place on 1/21/2007. Mr. Mayes never attacked or assaulted me as stated by the police in the police report. Mr. Mayes and I had a simple disagreement. I recommend that the charges be dropped because out of all the foolish things that Mr. Mayes does, I can honestly state that he is not a threat to our children or me and this is a huge waste of everyone's time. If you have further questions or concerns please contact me by mail or phone at (770) 899-1498.

Thank You,

Marlena Mayes

Even though the case was dropped, things were never the same between Charles and me. I found out he was cheating with two women that stayed in our apartment complex. I tried to beat the life out of one of the women. She was sleeping with him and grinning in my face the whole time when she knew we were married. We were going at it like cats and dogs. I knew that things were ending, so I decided to put our things in storage until I found another place to live. One of my neighbors offered my kids and me a place to stay in Thomasville Heights, a low-income housing project. I had heard about Thomasville Heights a few months back while watching the news because of a drive by shooting. A young boy was caught in the crossfire while trying to protect a little girl. Never in a million years would I ever have thought I would have to consider living there.

No sooner than we started moving, all hell broke loose. I found out that not only was Charles cheating with two of our neighbor's, he was cheating with another woman and her daughter happened to be good friends with my oldest daughter. They were extremely close. I was devastated. When things seemed like they couldn't get any worse, my car broke down and I got arrested in front of my children. I was arrested and charged with cruelty to children and disorderly conduct while trying to get a part for my car because I was caught chastising my children in public. I literally felt as if I had the weight of the world on my shoulders. I was under a tremendous amount of pressure and stress.

I struggled with everything that happened. I felt that part of the reason for my arrest had to do with race and the perception that the police officer had of me. I never would have been arrested for something so foolish if I were still living in Detroit. It replayed in my mind over and repeatedly. I was unaware that people could go to jail for something so foolish. The arrest cost me more than anyone could imagine. I had to spend 3 days in jail, I had to quit my job, I was denied public housing, I was not able to find another job, and my daughters are afraid of the police. I started going to counseling, church, and taking parenting classes to help deal with the guilt. This one incident had the extreme consequences and I did not deserve to be punished for something so foolish. I thought about Charles and how he felt when he was locked up. I also thought about what I was going to do to get my life in order once I got out. When I got out, I eventually wrote a letter to the judge explaining my side of the story.

State Court Of Dekalb County

To Whom It May Concern,

    I am writing this letter regarding case #07-071905. I was arrested June 3, 2007 at Pull-the-Part Auto for allegedly being cruel to my children, disorderly conduct, and obstructing an officer. Yelling at my children, being cruel to my children, or abusing my children is completely out of my character, but according to Officer Levy, he overheard me tell my daughter to go to the f***ing car &

some unidentified person witnessed me hit my daughter in public.

Under normal circumstances, I would have never been in a situation that appeared or resembled me being cruel to my children but this situation was much different. When I arrived at the Pull-the-Part Auto, it was about 30 minutes before closing time. The store was not crowded and Officer Levy was at the front door. I stopped at the front counter for assistance and I was directed by an employee to enter the yard for help. I asked a gentleman who was nearby for help and he agreed to help me until one of the employees drove up and informed us that children were not allowed on the yard and the store would be closing in 20 minutes. That was the first time that anyone mentioned to me that children were not allowed on the yard and once I was informed I immediately starting walking with my neighbor and my daughters back to the car and instructed my oldest daughter to remain with my neighbor until I came out of the store.

At that time my daughter stated that she wanted to stay with me she did not want to wait in the car. I told her she had to wait in the car. By this time we had reentered the store and my cell phone had rung. I answered my cell phone and proceeded to the checkout counter to find out if the part I was looking for was available and if so could it be put on hold. The next thing I knew the same employee was talking to Officer Levy. Officer Levy looked over at me.

I immediately told my daughter once again that she was going to have to get in the car with my neighbor and she said she wanted to stay with me. I do believe at this time I did tell my 8 year old daughter to just go to the f***ing car and without warning Officer Levy comes over and starts trying to handcuff me in front of my children. My cell phone was still in my hand and when I tried to hand my cell phone over to my daughter he forcefully tried to restrain me. My daughters started crying and I started pleading with them to take my phone and just go get in the car because I did not know what was going to happen. At this point, I informed him that he was hurting me and I was just trying to give my cell phone to my daughter. He told me that I could not talk to my daughter like that in public and he was placing me under arrest. The gentleman that originally helped me came over to Officer Levy trying to convince him to let me go, Officer Levy told the customer that if he did not leave he would arrest him also. My neighbor stood in the door way of the store trying to figure out what was going on and Officer Levy instructed her to take my kids and leave because he was placing me under arrest. After my neighbor left with my children, I asked Officer Levy again why he was arresting me and I informed him once again that I felt as if I really had not done anything wrong at least not anything to the point that I deserved to be arrested in front of my children. I tried to explain my position to Officer Levy but he disregarded everything I was telling him. Shortly thereafter, back up had arrived to transport me to jail and Officer Levy began to search and question me in front of Officer Logan, but I was in tears, complete disbelief, and I went in to shock. I did not act or react any different than anyone in my shoes would have done. I am an excellent parent regardless of how the situation may have seemed and I have numerous awards and honors to prove it. I have been an intricate part of my daughters' life. In addition, I am a hardworking, law abiding citizen that has witnessed everything I have accomplished be taken away from me because I now have a criminal arrest record. I am begging the court to review the attached information and dismiss my case.

Sincerely,
Marlena Mayes

This whole situation was very depressing and never in a billion years did I think Charles would do the things he did. I became very depressed and got to a point where I felt like I was better off dead than alive. Everything I worked for went down the drain. Everything that I cared about was one big disappointment. My kids didn't understand what was going on and why things had to change. My oldest daughter even wondered why I was so upset with her friend's mother and why all of us couldn't move in together and be one big happy family. At that point, I really felt like my life was over. I had a friend from out of town come stay with me and she even turned her back on me. She suggested that maybe it was me who ruined our marriage and for a moment, I thought that maybe she was right. I tried to figure out what I had done wrong. We had our difficulties before we got married but I never cheated or even thought of being with another man after we were married. I cooked, I cleaned, I worked, I would even sacrifice my own needs and wants to make sure that my family was taken care of and had what they needed. What was I doing wrong? I got depressed even thinking about how much I sacrificed to make things work so that I would not end up like my parents.

I was seriously depressed and I felt like I had no one to turn to. This was a huge turning point in my life. I cried out for help. I questioned my spirituality and my purpose for living. Just when I was ready to give up on everything I found a church home and had a spiritual awakening. Eventually I pulled myself together. In addition to me having a spiritual awakening there were several other things that helped me snap out of my depression so I listed 10 ways in which a person can deal with depression in a more effective manner. I hope this information helps someone. It's not easy dealing with depression but it can be done. I was determined to get past this and put everything behind me so once again, I kept moving forward and didn't give up.

How to deal with depression

1. Pray.
2. Get spiritual inspiration or motivation.
3. Meditate.
4. Reflect.
5. Rest.
6. Cut off contact with anyone or anything that is causing you to become depressed.
7. Take time out for yourself.
8. Take charge of your destiny.
9. Seek support from close friends, family or spiritual leaders.
10. Seek professional help.

CHAPTER 28

JUSTICE SERVED

I took my children back to live in Detroit with friends and family until my case was over. While I was there, I bought a car from my brother and drove it back down to Atlanta. I got a job working as a temporary worker. I worked as much as I could. I didn't have a place to stay at the time because things didn't work out in the housing projects. It wasn't any place that I could get use to living in anyway. I stayed in a room for a while. I even stayed with a mutual friend of Charles. She was real cool, she had two daughters and she was doing her best to support them.

I would still get depressed. I felt like I was at a low point in my life. I would go out from time to time hoping I would meet someone that would sweep me off my feet and be there for me the way that I was there for my husband. I missed cooking and having dinner together as a family. I missed having a home and doing things as a family. Nothing else mattered to me because everything I knew had disappeared overnight. My youngest daughter came back to live with me but my oldest daughter wanted to stay. I didn't blame her and I knew that was probably the best thing for her at the time. I thought about how my mother always put us off on other people so I hesitated at first, but eventually, I had no choice. School was starting and I had no permanent place of my own. Everyone said I should just move back, but I had this case pending and I had nothing to go back to.

I kept hoping and praying that my situation would change. I knew things had to change for the better because they couldn't get any worse. Charles couldn't help because his situation was worse than mine. He ended up leaving the girl he was cheating on me with for one of her friends. That whole situation was a mess. They weren't only friends but they were also co-workers. They were both waitresses at the Hard Rock Café. Every time I turned around, I was hearing about the drama he was going through. He was cheating on both of them and still married to me.

Even though I missed being together as a family, I was glad that I wasn't dealing with his foolishness anymore. After my turbulent upbringing, several failed relationships, and two children, I didn't know what else to do with myself. I felt so lost. I didn't want to seriously think about dating or meeting anyone new, but I refused to give up on meeting "Mr. Right." I tried going out and moving on with my life, but I wasn't happy, so I kept hoping and praying.

Just when I thought my luck couldn't get any worse, my car broke down again. My car was all that I had left so now, I really didn't know what to do. I was able to pull over into a service station before it completely cut off. I put my head down against the stirring wheel and prayed that things would get better. A man pulled up to help me. He was with his son and he didn't seem to know what he was doing. A second man pulled up shortly after and he was by himself. The second guy looked at the car and said my head gasket was blown. He was able to get the car started and offered to follow me to make sure I made it where I was going. His name was Warren and he was extremely handsome, so I didn't refuse. He gave me his number and told me to call him when I got in and got situated. I called him later on that evening but I didn't get an answer. I started thinking about my day and getting ready to go to sleep. I told myself that despite how the day started out, it ended okay. I said a silent prayer and no sooner than I closed my eyes, he called. It seemed like we talked forever and I felt like I knew him my whole life.

Shortly after our phone conversation, we went out with each other and from that point on, I knew that I didn't want to be with any other man. He was articulate and intelligent. He was self-made and had everything I thought I wanted in a man. He told me everything I wanted to hear and said he didn't want me to ever need anything from another man. We talked about my entire situation. He told me that he would be there for me and help me get back on my feet but I had to meet him half way and I agreed. I was a little reluctant about how fast things were developing between us because I didn't fully understand his situation. He told me he was divorced, he had an on and off again relationship with another woman that he had children by, but they were like two ships passing in the night. I didn't question his situation too much because legally, I was still married. I decided that I was just going to take things one day at a time and see where things went. He and I started seeing each other regularly, but it was mainly on the weekend because I worked during the week and so did he. Within a month of us dating, he paid for me to move into a new apartment. It was nice. It was a three bedroom, two-bathroom unit.

No sooner than I moved into the apartment, the court called. They said my case was diverted and I would not be prosecuted. I was relieved that the case was finally over and I could finally put this matter behind me. The memories of being locked up in jail made me think back over my childhood. I thought about how life was when I was institutionalized and in and out of different group homes. It was no fun being caged up like an animal. I finally felt like things were looking up for me.

I thought that getting on my feet and moving into a new place would really bring us closer together but it actually did the opposite. I expected him to start spending more time with me but he didn't. I would call him several times throughout the week, but he was working on a project or out of town. When he called me and wanted to see me, I was usually at work. He seemed to have a problem with me working, so I stopped working the temporary assignments and started working from home. He still wasn't satisfied or ever around when I expected him to be. I gave up and assumed that he was involved with someone else. I went out on a couple of occasions and when he found out, he was pissed. He didn't like me going out or the possibility of me meeting other men. I didn't take him seriously at first because I felt like as long as he was doing what he wanted to do, I was going to do what I wanted to do. From the time that we met and started dating, I honestly did not have an interest in seeing anyone else but him. My focus was getting my household in order and getting myself together so that I could be there for my kids. However, there was one particular incident when I felt like *to hell with him* and decided to invite a guy over to the apartment. Once again, when Warren found out, he was furious. It was like he had a radar. He happened to call while the guy was over and I did not want to lie or play games so I told him I had company. The next thing I knew, Warren was knocking at the door. Even though the guy and I were only sitting in the living room talking about some future business plans, Warren went off. From that point on, we had more in depth conversations about our involvement with each other and I tried to take him seriously. He made it clear that he didn't want me seeing anyone else or going out. He also made it clear that he didn't want to be dating a married woman so I needed to get a divorce, and I did. I didn't have much money so I prepared and filed the divorce papers by myself. The divorce was finalized about six months later.

I didn't know exactly where Warren and I stood, but we had been sexually involved with each other so I decided to get a physical and be tested for HIV. I had not been to the doctor in almost two years because I lost my health insurance. I was so nervous. A few nights of pleasure could change things for the rest of my life. I trusted Warren, but like I said before, I learned not to put anything past anyone. We connected so fast that I don't think either one of us had an opportunity to truly think about what was going on. Our chemistry felt right, but none of that would matter if these tests came back positive for anything. I wouldn't be able to trust him and he damn sure wouldn't be able to trust me. Warren was a good guy. I knew he did his dirt and made a few mistakes early in life, but he had a good heart. He was a real man and he accepted the consequences of his actions so I couldn't do anything but respect him. I felt like he would never do anything to put my life or his life in jeopardy but I had to be sure. All of my tests came back negative, but about two months later; I found out that I was pregnant. We talked about having children so I assumed that he was going to take the news well.

We had our ups and our downs during the first part of my pregnancy. He was skeptical about the baby being his at first because I went out with someone else. In addition to me going out with someone else, I had been telling him that I was unhappy and interested in seeing other people. We had a big argument one day when he found out I had been talking to one of the mothers of his children. He talked all kind of mess and acted as if I had betrayed him, but less than 24 hours later; he was calling my phone and knocking at the door. Regardless of what we went through, we never stayed mad at each other for long.

I had some very trying times during my pregnancy. Even though he would come around and always check on me, I was on my own for the most part. He was there if I needed him financially, but that was about it. I wasn't sure how one particular day was going to turn out because I had a dental appointment and a prenatal appointment scheduled for the same day. It wouldn't have been so bad if I still had a car but I didn't. Waiting on public transportation was starting to take a toll on me. I wouldn't dare ask Warren to take me anywhere I needed to go because I would have a better chance waiting on a pig to fly. I asked him to take me to the grocery store one time and I nearly starved to death because it took him 2 days. I asked him to bring me some food twice during my pregnancy and it took him 12 hours. It was not intentional; Warren was just slow and moved on his on time.

I never could get use to depending on people anyway. I could never understand how some women could get caught up or trapped in a relationship. I always said that it wouldn't be me. People moved at their own pace no matter who they were or how much you meant to them. That was something else I learned from my parents. Therefore, when it came to depending on a man, I understood that I was on my own until a man was ready to do for me.

I wasn't going to complain too much because things were worse with Charles. He did what he wanted when he wanted. In our divorce agreement, he was ordered to pay around $270 a month for child support but he never paid a dime. Then he had the nerve to wonder why I was asking him for money as if he expected our daughter to raise herself. I stopped dealing with him all together and accepting his calls. If he wanted to see his daughter, he had to make an appointment. He was a deadbeat, but let him tell it, he was father of the year. He did more while we were married, but I would have been a fool if I had remained married to him.

How to deal with divorce

1. Stop feeling guilty.

2. Stay active.

3. Analyze your feelings.

4. Take care of yourself.

5. Spend time with yourself.

6. Spend time with your friends and family.

7. Lose the "You Owe Me" attitude.

8. Analyze your finances and plan

   accordingly.

9. Choose your battles wisely.

10. Seek professional help if necessary.

Divorce is a very touchy subject. I was devastated when my ex-husband and I first separated. It had very little to do with him, it was more about my kids and having to start over after we had been together for so many years. I worked so hard and invested so much time and energy into our marriage. Dealing with divorce is difficult for most people so I listed 10 ways in which a person can deal with divorce in an effective manner.

As far as Warren and I were concerned, we continued to have a few ups and downs, but we always made it through them. He was firmly planted in my life and regardless of what we went through; he assured me that he wasn't going anywhere. I wanted us to have a more traditional relationship because I always valued being in a committed relationship and having a family, but I refused to put any pressure on him. I told myself that if it were truly meant to be, it would be.

CHAPTER 29

THE PROUD &ARROGANT MAN

The further along I got in my pregnancy, the more involved Warren got. He started coming around more and spending more time with me. I started purchasing things for the baby. The only person that was missing was my oldest daughter but it wouldn't be long before she was back with me. I hated pulling her from school, family and friends in Detroit but I felt like apart of me was missing since she had been gone. I felt bad because I was preparing for the baby and I wasn't able to provide for her financially. I knew that I was missing an intricate part of her life. She had been away from me for about a year but it seemed like forever. We talked all the time but I didn't want to tell her about the baby until Warren and I was able to tell her together. She, however, kept me well informed on everything that was going on in her life. We saw each other on breaks and during the holidays. At the end of the school year, she finally came back to live with me.

I was happy for a moment and things were going ok, but I still felt alone. One day, I sat back and contemplated all the qualities and characteristics that I was looking for in my ideal mate. I concluded that I wanted a man that is spiritually grounded, respectful, business driven, financially stable, mentally supportive, and goal-oriented. I expected my ideal mate to be in good health and mentally supportive. Last, but not least, I wanted someone that was willing to love me for me and unconditionally. Although I loved Warren beyond belief and I felt that he was the epitome of what a man should be, he wasn't in love with me and he didn't treat me the way in which I wanted to be treated. I knew that he loved me but he was not in love with me. He was still holding on and trying to make past relationships work for the benefit of his other children. I never expected him to walk away from his responsibilities and start a life with me, but I did expect him to understand that I wanted to be in a monogamous relationship and if that was not what we were working towards, then our involvement with each other had to end.

I told myself the next time I got into a serious relationship; I would do a few things differently. I made a list of things that I felt were important like making sure my potential mate and I closed out all of our past relationships with a good understanding. I would like us to know each other's basic needs before we start planning a life together or even start talking about marriage. I don't want to have rules and set up boundaries, but I do think it is important that we discuss each others place and role in the relationship. I'm a modern day woman with old fashion beliefs and I believe that a woman's primary responsibility is to take care of her home and her children. I believe that a woman should work around her family's obligations, but a man is supposed to provide for his family's basic needs. Establishing a budget and disclosing where each of us stand credit wise is important to me. We would definitely have to have a prenuptial agreement and attend premarital counseling.

Despite everything that I had gone through in my previous marriage, I wanted to get married again. I valued having a family and being domestic. The ceremony or process was not of importance to me. My concern was more or less with making a commitment to the person that I cared about. I was tired of dating and I definitely was not interested in meeting someone new. I knew that one day I would find the person that was meant for me, but until that time came, I was going to focus on managing my time and household duties by myself. I decided that I was going to stop neglecting myself and start managing my time more wisely. I created a schedule for the children and myself. I try to stick to the schedule as close as possible. Although my activities and appointments varied from day to day, I used my schedule as a general guideline for all the things I needed to do throughout the day. Most of my work or appointments were during normal business hours. I tried to refrain from obligating myself to anything that would take too much time away from my kids or household responsibilities. This caused problems for me in the past, especially in my marriage, so I didn't want it to be an issue for me again.

I included my schedule and a list of ways people can manage their time more efficiently, in hope that this information will be valuable or useful to others. Managing my time became extremely important when I realized how much time was slipping away from me. I wasted a lot of time on relationships that I never should have been in to begin with however I believe that people were brought into my life for a reason. I gained valuable lessons from each one of those relationships and I realized that I had to stop waiting or expecting a man to come into my life and make me happy. Companionship and having a family was only one aspect of my happiness. I began to accept the fact that I can have the family I want without necessarily having a man. I had to continue moving forward and setting higher goals. Although I had been through a lot and accomplished a lot, I felt as if I was capable of doing so much more, so I set new goals and priorities for myself.

Schedule

Daily Routine	Time
Pray	6:00am
Review daily activities	6:15am
Exercise	6:30am
Wash face, brush teeth, floss & rinse	6:45am
Wrap hair & take shower	7:00am
Put on body oils & clothes	7:15am
Put on make-up & do hair	7:30am
Breakfast	7:45am
Clean up & make beds	8:00am
Complete daily activities & work	9:00am
Prepare dinner	6:00pm
Spend time with the kids	7:00pm
Clean up	8:00pm
Take evening shower	8:30pm
Wash face, brush teeth, floss & rinse	8;45pm
Put on body oils & night clothes	9:00pm
Set out clothes for next day	9:15pm
Write out schedule for next day	9:30pm
Relax & meditate	9:45pm
Pray	10:00pm

How to manage your time

1. Plan a head.

2. Always remember, "The early bird gets the worm" so start your days early.

3. Write out a list.

4. Have a daily schedule.

5. Don't procrastinate.

6. Don't over-extend yourself.

7. Set priorities.

8. Multi-task.

9. Divide your time into 10 or 15-minute increments.

10. Track your progress.

CHAPTER 30

AN AXIOUS HEART WEIGHS A MAN D OWN

I wasn't sure what lied ahead for me over the next year, but I knew things would hopefully get better. This country's economy was a mess. I was somewhat hopeful because for the first time in my life, we had two distinctly different candidates campaigning for the democratic nomination and they both had an excellent chance of becoming the next president.

I kept up with everything that was going on in the news, especially politics. That was one of the characteristics that Warren and I had in common. One of the other characteristics that we had in common is that we both loved to talk, we could talk for hours. Even though I decided to stop seeking companionship and a commitment from him, we had a child on the way so our friendship remained a priority to me.

I was still very much head over heels in love with him. The way I felt about him was much different from anything I ever experienced before. I don't know what attracted me to him. He had this arrogant self-consumed, self-absorbed side, but he was also very caring and emotional. We had similar pasts and got along extremely well. I catered to him whenever he came by the apartment. I tried to be his friend by uplifting him and restoring his energy when he got discouraged, depressed, or started feeling heavy. I tried to be there for him financially, even if it meant loaning him my last when I knew that he was in a better financial situation than me. I provided him with the space, time, and freedom he needed without making demands, saying bad things about him, or hunting him down when I knew he was probably with other women. The only thing that I concerned myself with was making sure that I was a good person and there for him to the best of my ability when he needed me.

I believed in him because he believed in me when I was ready to give up on myself. He pulled me up and restored my heart when it was torn to pieces. Regardless of where our friendship went, we were looking forward to bringing a child into the world together. We had our difficulties, which was normal for most expecting parents. When this happened, I didn't make a big deal about the situation or get all emotional, I would simply give us some space.

I continued focusing on my kids, preparing for the baby, and I even started writing. I thought about my life and decided to write a book. I went through all my old things and all of my old love letters. Although I was doing well on the outside, I started to cry as I reflected upon everything that happened throughout my life. For some reason, David and his letters stayed on my mind. A few days passed by and I kept thinking about him, so I decided to look him up. I suspected that he had probably been released or paroled, but to my surprise, he was still locked up. I got the address and decided to write him. When I was finished writing the letter, it stayed on my dresser for a few days before I finally got enough courage to mail it. Warren knew that I planned to write him. He didn't like it but he couldn't say much. A letter arrived in the mail from David about a week later.

Dear Marlena

First, let me start off by saying that though unexpected, I was more than happy to hear from you. Hearing that you are doing as well as it seems is just icing on the cake and I sincerely pray that your success in anything that you apply yourself at continues.

Without you making mention of it too much I can only believe that you are a beautiful and wonderful mother. And as far as your relationship goes just let me express that deep down I am a tad bit jealous. I must admit that even though so much time (13 + years) without hearing from you. I'm still stirring in the inside even after reading your letter 3 times.

In all honesty, it hasn't been more than a week since I was telling someone about you and how I would love to hear from you. Maybe my desire is the cause for your compulsion to write. Fate does have a way of causing things to be.

As far as I go, despite my placement I'm at a great place in my life, spiritually, mentally and physically. And though nothing right now is certain, I should be home sometime next year (GOD willing). My plans are a little murky right now but I believe I have a couple of things to fall back on.

I also began a book but felt I lacked the overall life experience to finish it the way I wanted to. It is a semi autobiographic book in which a young man not long released from prison is torn between living a life of uplift or once again becoming a tool for destruction. After being home for a while and establishing my finances and home life it is my goal to finish it.

Marlena, I thoroughly understand your situation and all but I must say I'm very excited hearing from you and I hope that continues in any capacity.

Sincerely,
David

I tried to keep my friendship with David mutual. Any thoughts of us being together were quickly blocked out of my mind because I had been down this road before and I wasn't eager to go back. Besides everything that had went on between us in the past, I had a lot going on. The lease was almost up on the apartment. It just so happened that a close friend asked could she come stay with me because she was going through a few changes. I thought it would be good because I needed help with the kids since the baby was on the way.

Warren encouraged me to look for a house. About a month before our son was scheduled to be born, I moved into the house. When things seemed liked they were starting to fall into place for me, things ultimately fell apart for Warren. He lost a very close friend, then he lost his uncle, and his mother was diagnosed with breast cancer. I tried to be there for him emotionally, but at times, I felt like he was shutting me out so as usual, I gave us some space.

David and I continued writing and talking to each other over the phone. We would oftentimes talk about my relationship with Warren and my pregnancy. I gained some relief by being able to talk about things and hear things from a male perspective. Our letters and conversations actually turned out a lot differently then I expected them to. I had my own stereotypical beliefs and assumptions that since he had been in jail so long that he might be gay, bisexual or a lot different than I knew him to be. To my surprise, many things were very much the same and the few things about him that had changed, had changed for the better.

I valued my friendship with David, but my heart was still with Warren. Even though I felt like he was shutting me out, I told myself I was still going to be there for him when he needed me. The end of my pregnancy was quickly approaching and I was focused on getting adjusted to the new house. No sooner than everything was settled in the house, I woke up one morning in a puddle of water. I tried not to panic and remain calm, but after calling Warren a few times, I started to worry.

I didn't have a way to the hospital so I called one of my former neighbors from my old apartment complex to take me. She was cool and always looking out for me when she could. I would keep her kids and she would keep mine. We got to the hospital in no time. I was admitted and sent to a room. I got a call from Warren around midday and he came to the hospital that evening. I wasn't dilated far enough so the nurse inserted something into my cervix to help me along. It took about 24 more hours until I was fully ready to deliver. I was somewhat worried because Warren had left several hours earlier, but to my relief, he showed right before our son was delivered. I was so relieved when he finally arrived because it seemed like I was pregnant forever. He was so precious and such a sight to see. I loved all of my children and being a mother was one of the most rewarding feelings. I stayed in the hospital for a couple more days then I was quickly discharged. I came home the weekend before Thanksgiving. I was excited because one of my sisters was flying in from Houston. I was in no condition to be moving around, but I wanted to have a happy Thanksgiving. Things were going ok until all hell broke loose. Several kids came over my house during Thanksgiving break and some heartless woman called the police because the kids went to the park by themselves. Under normal circumstances, the children would not have gone to the park by themselves, but I was so focused on taking care of my newborn and trying to recover from having the baby, that I didn't monitor the situation. I knew that I had more than enough help, especially since my friend and her boyfriend had temporarily moved in with me. They were accustomed to helping out. They had managed to make sure things went well while I was in the hospital and we had a conversation the day before about them continuing to help out while I recovered. I was overwhelmed and oblivious as to how things fell apart that day. I was stressed out and pissed off, but I was ready to deal with whatever came my way. None the less, the police came to my house and I was eventually arrested. I stayed in jail for about 12 hours until Warren came and bonded me out. My bond was $7000, but he ended up paying a bails bondsmen $1300 to get me out. I was furious and didn't know what to do. I was worried the whole time that I was in jail about being away from my kids, especially my son since he was nursing.

I was relieved when I finally made it home, but it was the holiday season and I was not looking forward to a long drawn out court case. Warren made things a lot easier on me while I was going through everything. He helped me get a truck and then gave me $2000 to help with my bills. I applied for an attorney with the public defenders office. I assumed they were probably backed up with other frivolous cases because my court date was approaching and I hadn't been assigned an attorney yet so I decided to write a letter.

Friday, February 13, 2009
State Court Of Cobb County Georgia
State Court Building, Courtroom D3
21 East Park Circle
Marietta, Georgia 30090-9670

Judge Carl,

My name is Marlena Mayes and I am writing this letter in regards to case #09-M-42D 08-W-14081. According to court documents, the State of Georgia is charging me with 11 counts of Reckless Conduct 16-5-60 a Misdemeanor. The document further states that "I was allegedly operating an unlicensed daycare from my home and unlawfully endangered the bodily safety of another person: a child under the age of 16 by consciously disregarding a substantial and unjustifiable risk and my actions were such a disregard as to constitute a gross deviation from the standard of care which a reasonable person would exercise in the situation." **At this time, I would like to state the facts and request that the case be dismissed because it is unjust and frivolous.**

The court case stems from an incident that took place during the week of Thanksgiving, November 25, 2009 when 13 children and 4 adults were at my home. 11 of the children allegedly walked two blocks (less than a half of mile) to the park without adult supervision. A daycare owner by the name of Lisa M. Abernathy called the police and had the children taken into police custody.

Under normal circumstances, 13 children would not be at my home nor would any of them have walked to the park alone without adult supervision, but I made an error in judgment by entrusting the care of my children and the other children visiting my home during Thanksgiving recess to someone else while I was recovering from giving birth to my son and getting settled into my new home (please see attached hospital discharge form and lease agreement).

It is my strong belief that the charges against me are unfair, unreasonable, and unjust because I took every reasonable measure to make sure that proper care was provided for my children, as well as the children that were visiting my home. The severity of the matter and situation was greatly over exaggerated. I have over 10 years of experience in childcare. All of the children that were visiting my home have an ongoing relationship with my children and come to my home frequently. Our children participate in activities together, spend the night at each other's home, and are welcome to play with each other at any time.

I do understand that endangering the life of another human being, especially a child is a serious matter and I am deeply saddened by the minor incident that took place, but I do; however, feel that I have been punished enough because I had to spend a day in jail away from my newborn and other children. I was investigated by the Department of Family and Children Services until the case was closed. I was also investigated by the State of Georgia's Bright from the Start Program for two weeks. I have been reprimanded more than I can take. I was under the impression that the children were being supervised at the children park. When I found out the children was alone I got up to go find out about the children but by that time it was too late because the police had already taken them into custody. The entire incident took place in less than 30 minutes. If I could have done anything differently I would have but I really did not have an opportunity to rectify the situation.

I am pleading with the court to have a little bit of empathy, compassion, consideration, or mercy towards me because I just had a baby 12 weeks ago and I took every reasonable measure to ensure that the kids in my home were properly cared for while I recovered. I am a pillar in my community, aspiring entrepreneur, and an excellent parent. My daughter is an excellent student and has never missed a day of school. I have been honored and won numerous awards for my volunteer work. The three parents of the other children involved in the incident have provided character witness statements for me and they have no interest in prosecuting me (please see attached information). Although I cannot undo what has already been done or place the blame on anyone but myself, I have learned a lot from this incident and I will take greater precautions in the future.

Sincerely,
Marlena Mayes

Warren continued to stand by me the whole time while I was going through the court case. Our personal relationship had not improved that much, there was always drama between him and the mothers of his other children. I tried to stay out of it and accept the fact that he was there when I needed him most. Warren knew that David and I talked frequently but it wasn't much that he could say. I tried to keep my friendship with David on a certain level, but the harder I tried, the more my feelings started to redevelop for him.

I really didn't know what to do as far as my personal life was concerned because I felt like my freedom was on the line. The court didn't respond to my letter but I was finally assigned a defense attorney. When I met with him at his office, he said things were not looking too good for me. The solicitor's office and prosecutor was only offering me jail time. Warren eventually said we needed to hire an attorney so that is what we did. My new attorney got me a much better deal. Instead of 1 year in jail, I was looking at 1-year probation, a fine, parenting class, and community service, but I felt like the case should have been dropped all together.

On the day that I had to go to court, I didn't want to get out of bed for some strange reason, even though my case was being resolved. I woke up running late because I didn't go to bed until after midnight when I knew I needed to wake up at the crack of dawn. I got up at 5:00am to feed my son, but I couldn't convince myself that it was time to start my day, so I laid back down. No sooner than I rolled over to look at the clock, I realized that I had over slept.

When I arrived at court, I was running late and ready to get the whole thing over with; but to my surprise the courtroom was almost empty and my attorney was not present. I knew something was wrong, but I tried to fight the feeling and tell myself that everything was going to be all right. I approached the court clerk and she stated that my attorney called and he was running late because he was tied up in another courtroom. I was relieved but something still didn't feel right. I sat and watched the Judge and everyone else that was in the courtroom laugh, joke, and play around. I guess the Judge realized that I was taking notice and made an announcement that if my attorney wasn't here by 10:30am; he was going to postpone the matter. I was getting annoyed at this point. My last attorney didn't show up until after court was over and this attorney was on the verge of doing the same thing. If it weren't for bad luck, I felt like I probably wouldn't have any at all. I seriously believed that someone must have put a curse on me.

I called my attorney's office and they said not to worry because my attorney was on is way. Next, I called Warren to let him know what was going on. No sooner than I came back in the courtroom and sat down on the bench, my attorney came storming in. The prosecutor asked if she could see him in the Judge's chambers. I could tell that something was wrong. The bad feeling I had earlier got even worse and all I could do was pray that they wouldn't try to hang me. I didn't care because either way, I was going to be ok. If it wasn't for my kids, I honestly would have opted to do the time because I was tired of the whole court situation. I was in and out of family court my entire life, so this situation wasn't going to make much of a difference. I started getting pissed thinking about how the system had failed me my entire life, now I was hemmed up in court for the second time on some mess waiting to see if my freedom would be taken.

Just as I suspected, this mess wasn't over and this case was going to be dragged out for another three months because the judge and everyone else was worried about my letter and how this case would look to the media. When my attorney told me that I had to come back in three months, I wanted to act a damn fool. This was my life that they were playing around with and they were more worried about their political career. The justice system had never managed to be on my side. I tried to be a law-abiding citizen and stay out of trouble my whole life but that day, I felt like going postal. Warren showed up to the courtroom just as my attorney and I were walking out and it's a good thing he did because if he hadn't, I was probably going to end up in jail. He calmed me down long enough for us to get out of the courthouse without making too much of a scene. We went across the street to the park to talk. He told me his whole life story for the one-millionth time and let me know that I would get through this. He told me that he believed in me and knew I was a good person with a good heart that unfortunately ended up in a bad situation. This was the first time in a while that we were able to have a heart to heart talk. After we were done talking, we went and sat down for something to eat. As soon as we started eating, David called. Unbeknownst to me, Warren reached across the table and answered the phone. I could only imagine what David was thinking on the other end. I felt bad because I knew that David was going to call to check on me. This was actually the second or third time that they had exchanged words over the phone and both of them knew about each other from the beginning so I didn't feel like I owed either one of them an explanation.

Warren took the situation better than I assumed he would, but it was far from over. He used my involvement with David as an excuse to continue carrying on his relationships with the mothers of his other children. I didn't have a problem with him carrying on with the mothers of his other children as long as he was not trying to carry on with me at the same time. I wanted him to take care of our son and leave it at that. Warren loved all of his children and wanted to be an intricate part of each one of their lives, but he was also used to being in power and having control. It seemed that as long as he was fulfilling his financial obligations to his children, he felt as if he had the right to control the mothers of his children. I refused to get caught up or trapped in that type of situation so I decided that I was slowly going to regain my independence.

I started looking for reasons not to deal with him anymore so that I could be done with him once and for all without any regrets. I wanted to be able to feel like I had lived up to my end of the bargain and it was he that didn't want to act right. I even started distancing myself from David and focusing on goals and objectives that I had set for myself. I was presently surprised that although I was looking for reasons not to deal with Warren, our relationship actually started to improve until I found out he had a little girl that was about 3 months younger than our son. I knew of the other woman. He was involved with her before he got involved with me. They didn't have any children together at the time. I found out about her after talking to his child's mother and I told myself that was it. I was packing up my things and finally going to move back to Detroit.

I moved out of my house, put my things in storage, and made a list of the other things that I needed to do before I left Georgia. The only thing that I had to worry about was showing back up for court, finding a place in Detroit, and finding a job so that I could get on my feet. I found out that David was going to be paroled. Even though we had not seen each other in so many years, I wanted to be there when he came home.

I planned to leave for Detroit as soon as Jada got out of school for the summer. I knew that Warren was going to talk me out of moving back to Detroit, but it was nothing that he could say to make me stay. I was tired and I wanted to be done. I was ready to start living for my children and me. I was tired of stressing out over things that I literally had no control over. My life was like an emotional rollercoaster. I knew what I had to do to get myself together, I was just too afraid to do it.

I went to Detroit, but of course, things didn't continue going like I had planned. I spent the whole summer traveling to and from Detroit with the kids. I applied for a few jobs and worked on a couple of projects, but I didn't feel comfortable moving back. I felt like I had been moved around my whole life and I knew in my heart that I was moving for the wrong reason. Tension grew between me and Warren, especially when he found out that David got paroled. He felt like I betrayed him and walked away from what we had. He went through a complete emotional outcry phase and he almost had me going for a moment. He made all types of promises and plans. He promised to help me with my book, help me pay for nursing school, and he even promised to marry me once I finished school. I found out that I was pregnant again with our second child but I wasn't going to sit back and wait on him to live up to his promises. I had to do what was best for me. I had to do it on my own, keep pushing forward and live out my destiny.

How to live your destiny

1. Break through barriers.

2. Realize you're potential.

3. Realize your inevitable fate.

4. Live a balanced life.

5. Make the most out of every situation.

6. Build your faith.

7. Take charge of your life.

8. Set goals and achieve them.

9. Keep your dreams alive.

10. Remember, "There is nothing to it but to do it."

Life is hard but no one ever said that it is supposed to be easy. As we struggle with finding our purpose or place in life, we must remember that our destiny was predetermined before we entered the world. We will either fail or succeed in life. Those are the only 2 options. I refuse to fail and plan to overcome anything that stands in my way. I listed 10 ways in which a person can maximize their potential and live out their destiny in hopes that someone will avoid making some of the foolish mistakes that I have made and be influenced to make a difference.

EPILOGUE

DESTINY

Even after all the damage was done, Warren and I remained close, but there was no guarantee that we would ever settle down together and get married. David and I also kept in touch from time to time. He started dating other people. We took our friendship one day at a time. I focused on uplifting my children, myself, and inspiring the people around me. I tried to stop worrying about things I had no control over.

Everything happens for a reason. Nothing happens by coincidence. Like I said before, I am a firm believer that I was specifically designed by a higher power to persevere and make a difference. That is part of my destiny. I have very little, if any time left to make the same mistakes repeatedly. That is why I am doing things different the next time around. Being self disciplined and managing my time wisely was two of the most valuable lessons that I learned throughout my life. I just wish I knew the importance of those lessons before I made some of the mistakes that I made; but what's done is done. I cannot change the past and even if I could, I am not sure that I would want to. I am who I am because of the mistakes that I made.

No one ever said life was supposed to be easy, so I learned to get that thought out of my head a long time ago. Nothing comes easy and if it does, you will pay for it later. I had to learn that lesson the hard way. I am an adult now. I have no problem admitting my faults or admitting where I went wrong, but in the end, I knew things would work out for the best.

Out of all the experiences, people, and things that have influenced me, I have been my biggest influence. I made my own choices in life and I have to accept the responsibility for my mistakes, as well as the rewards for my accomplishments. My faith was and always will be very strong, so ultimately, my belief and faith in a higher power will be the biggest factor that determines how my life will play out. GOD is on my side and that is all that matters to me. Apparently, there are still times when I unintentionally go against my beliefs, conscience, and faith. Those are the times, when my flesh becomes weak and I allow distractions to overpower my better judgment. It is natural because like they say, no one is perfect and we all fall short of GOD's glory.

Each of us has a weakness or something that influences us or persuades us to give in. For one person, it may be alcohol, for another person, it may be drugs, but as for me; it was the fear of being alone. My turbulent upbringing and the things that I experienced in life influenced me and led me to believe that I needed people. My parents weren't in my life the way that I needed them to be so I tried to compensate by having a man. Yes, we need companionship and yes, we need people to a certain extent, but sometimes we need to learn how to love ourselves before we can expect anyone else to love us. It's been over 10 years since I have talked to my mother and it hurts. She turned her back and walked away from every last one of her children. My relationship with my father isn't too much better because I harbor some resentment towards him for everything that happened in the past and for not setting a better example of how a man should treat a lady. I don't like being alone and facing the world by myself. My heart desperately desires a life partner but I have to do what I have to do until the right person comes along. In the meantime, I am trying to overcome my fears and make better decisions. I try to make sure I utilize my full potential and the gifts that I have been blessed with because I am here to do GOD's work. My daughters are doing well and becoming accustomed to their new life. My son is growing and experiencing all that life has to offer. I am taking things day by day, learning to love life and myself as I await the arrival of my next little one. What more could a person ask for? Knowing what I want out of life helps me stay focused. It took me some time to figure it out and of course, I am still learning as I go, but I know that I am destined to do many great things. This life is not mine so I could not give up now even if I wanted to. Tomorrow is not promised. We are on borrowed time so we might as well make the most of it.

After Thoughts

Now that I have shared most of my life story with you, reflect back over your life. What is the most valuable lesson that you have learned throughout your life? What is the most valuable lesson that you have learned from reading *Influenced by Destiny*? Use the next several pages of this book to take notes and write about your own life experiences. Also use the next several pages write about your destiny and what has influenced you.

*Notes*_____

_____

_____

_____

_____

_____

*Notes*_____

----

*Notes*_____

----

*Notes*_____

_____

_____

_____

_____

_____

_____

_____

_____

_____

_____

_____

_____

_____

_____

_____

*Notes*_____

----

*Notes*_____

ABOUT THE AUTHOR

Marlena is a native Detroiter. She has a Bachelor's Degree in communications, Master's Degree in business and she is pursuing her Doctorate's Degree in education. She is the proud parent of four wonderful children. She enjoys assisting others, cooking, public speaking, raising her children, reading, shopping, and traveling. She currently resides in Atlanta, Georgia where she is working on her next book, working on a reality show, continuing her education, managing a non-profit organization, Ladies of Virtue and Excellence, Inc. and a publishing company, Prodigy Publishing, LLC.

For additional information about the author please visit www.marlenaneal.net. To schedule a speaking engagement, an empowerment workshop or training seminar, please call Prodigy Publishing, LLC at (877) 448-2349 or visit us on the web at www.prodigypublishings.com.

Support Prodigy Publishing LLC by ordering upcoming titles on-line at *www.marlenaeneal.com*, by calling 1(877)448-2349 or by completing the order form below.

Order Form

Name	
Address	
City State Zip	
Phone #	
Email	

Title	Quantity	Price
Influenced by Destiny 2		$14.95
Influenced by Success		$14.95
Influenced by Sex		$14.95
Influenced by the Streets		$14.95
Influenced By Violence		$14.95
Influenced by the Media		$14.95
Influenced by Music		$14.95
Influenced by Law		$14.95
Influenced by Corporate America		$14.95
Total		

Orders will be processed upon receipt of payment. Please allow 7-10 business days for turnaround time on all orders. Please mail order form along with a check or money orders to:

Prodigy Publishing LLC
2778 Cumberland Blvd #178
Atlanta, GA 30080-3048